100 CARD GAMES
for all the family

100 CARD GAMES
for all the family
HOURS OF FUN FOR PLAYERS OF ALL AGES

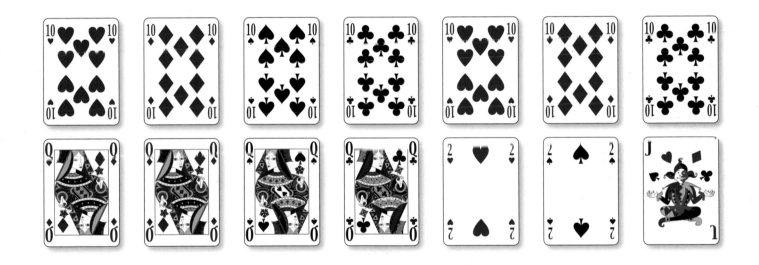

Jeremy Harwood

southwater

This edition is published by Southwater
an imprint of Anness Publishing Ltd
Blaby Road, Wigston, Leicestershire LE18 4SE
info@anness.com

www.southwaterbooks.com
www.annesspublishing.com

Anness Publishing has a new picture agency outlet
for images for publishing, promotions or advertising.
Please visit our website www.practicalpictures.com
for more information.

Designed and produced for Anness Publishing by
THE BRIDGEWATER BOOK COMPANY LIMITED

Publisher: Joanna Lorenz
Editorial Director: Helen Sudell
Editor: Joy Wotton
Production Controller: Helen Wang

Previously published as part of a larger volume,
How to Play 200 Card Games

PUBLISHER'S NOTE
Although the advice and information in this book are believed to be
accurate and true at the time of going to press, neither the authors nor
the publisher can accept any legal responsibility or liability for any errors
or omissions that may have been made nor for any inaccuracies nor for
any loss, harm or injury that comes about from following instructions or
advice in this book.

Anness Publishing would like to thank the following for kindly supplying
photographs for this book:
Alamy 8 (br), 25 (tr), 30 (br), 64 (bl).
Bridgeman Art Library 16 (br), 22 (cl), 24 (br), 62 (br),
92 (br), 119 (br).
BBco 2.
Corbis 6 (tr), 7 (tr), 95 (t), 96 (tr), 98 (bl, br), 121 (tr).
Dover Publications Inc. 8 (tl), 16 (tl), 24 (tl), 30 (tl), 40 (tl), 48 (tl), 62 (tl),
76 (tl), 92 (tl), 100 (tl), 106 (tl), 116 (bl), 119 (tl).
iStockphotography 43 (br), 76 (br), 78 (br), 128 (t).
Mary Evans Picture Library 7.
The Picture Desk 6 (bl), 7 (bl), 40 (br), 50 (tr), 100 (br), 106 (br), 121 (tr).
Robert Abbot 48 (br).

All artwork by Virginia Zeal

Every effort has been made to obtain permission to reproduce copyright
material, but there may be cases where we have been unable to trace the
copyright holder. The publisher will be happy to correct any omissions in
future printings.

CONTENTS

INTRODUCTION

The world of card games is endlessly fascinating. There are games available to suit practically any taste or age. Some are intuitive; others are intellectually challenging. Nearly all card games are action-packed and speedy. Unlike board games, most card games do not keep their players hanging on in suspense waiting for their turn to come around. To help you choose the best games for your family, all the games in this book have a suggested suitable age range from 4 years up to 14+.

PATIENCE AND SOLITAIRE GAMES

Card games for a single player are generically termed Patience in Europe and Solitaire in America. Playing them successfully demands clear thinking and concentration during play. David Parlett, the British card authority, described such games as 'the mental equivalent of jogging'.

Typically, the aim in solitaire games is to play out all the cards in the pack by arranging them in a specific order – usually in suit sequences, starting with the Ace and leading up to the King. When this is accomplished, the game is said to have 'come out'.

TRICK-TAKING GAMES

For many people the attraction of cards lies in playing against other players. Outplay games, as they are termed by experts, make up by far the largest category of card games. Each player is dealt a hand of cards, and each in turn plays one or more cards to the table. The game ends when one or all players run out of cards to play.

Above: A 17th-century French painting (artist unknown) depicting the making of playing cards, reproduced by means of hand-coloured woodcuts.

Above: A child turns up a card in the hope of finding a match in the Memory game, a quintessential family game that tests card-recall skills.

Most outplay games are trick-taking games, in which each player in turn plays a card face up to the table. This round of cards is called 'making a trick', and playing the first card is termed 'leading'. The card that wins the trick is either the highest of the suit originally led, or, if 'trumps' (cards of a suit nominated to be of higher value) are played, the highest card of that trump suit. Winning a trick often wins that round of cards and allows that player to choose which suit to lead next.

The way in which the trump suit is selected varies. In some games, the choice of trumps is random. They are selected by cutting the deck and exposing a card, usually at the end of the deal. In other games, the winner of the auction – in which the players bid against each other to make a certain number of tricks or points – decides what the trump suit is to be. Winning the right to choose trumps is therefore a powerful incentive in encouraging players to bid.

There are two ways of scoring such games. In what are termed point-trick games, the value of the tricks is affected by which cards they contain. The players are rewarded or penalized for capturing certain cards, each one of which has a pre-assigned value. This type of game includes Manille. In plain-trick games such as Ombre, on the other hand, it is only the number of tricks taken that matters. Play ends when some or all of the players run out of cards, at which point scores are totalled. The winner places the trick face down on the table and leads to the next trick. In games such as Piquet, the aim is both to win tricks and to score for card combinations.

NON-TRICK GAMES

Many card games are based on principles other than the taking of tricks. Some are children's classics, passed down through generations, and many are for adults, but they are all worth investigating. For example, Cribbage, an adding-up game, is a popular game for young people to play with their grandparents or older relatives.

In catch and collect games, the objective is to capture all the cards. Games such as Snap and Happy Families are simple children's games, while others such as Gops are far more complex. Fishing games such as Casino are particularly appealing. They are matching games in which each player competes to match the cards in hand with the ones laid out face up on the table. If the cards match, they are placed face down in front of the player who captured them. If there is no match, the card that was played is added to the layout on the table.

In shedding games, such as Michigan, the object is to get rid of all the cards as quickly as possible or to avoid being the last player holding cards. In collecting games, the object is to collect sets of matched cards (melds). The most popular of such games is Rummy – specifically, Gin Rummy, whose popularity stems from the fact that, while it is simple to pick up, play can become very skilled. Rummy-type games are also known as draw and discard games, because each player tries to improve his hand through drawing and discarding.

In banking games, such as Blackjack and Baccarat, an element of gambling is introduced. One player, the banker, takes on each of the other players individually to see who has the best hand. There is no need to play for money – use counters or candies.

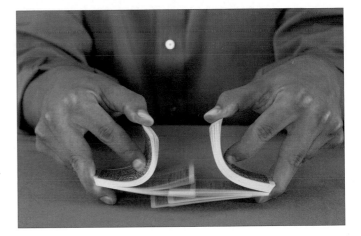

Above: Card play has a long-established set of procedures amounting almost to ritual. The shuffle is among them – it cannot be taught in words, only copied from watching good practitioners.

PLAYING THE GAME

Card-playing is entertaining for all the family. Many children enjoy playing games, following the rules – and making sure that the adults keep to them. Although card-playing involves many rules, they are worth following because they are prevent anyone having an unfair advantage. Set the rules at the beginning of the game, and make sure everyone understands them. It is customary to shuffle and cut the cards before each deal.

Make the game fun and family friendly by playing for counters, buttons, tokens or candies. Decide before you start playing what the penalties are for cheating, and at what point the game will cease (after a target score is reached or after a number of deals, for example). When choosing a game to play, look for one that suits the number of players and their card-playing abilities.

Far left: A 19th-century playing card trimmer (*c.*1870). Early playing cards were printed on uncoated stock and were occasionally trimmed to eliminate the frayed edges.

Left: *The Illustrated Book of Patience Games* by Angelo Lewis (a.k.a. Professor Hoffman), published in 1917 and reprinted several times.

1 | PATIENCE AND SOLITAIRE GAMES

PATIENCE GAMES, KNOWN AS SOLITAIRE GAMES IN THE USA, FALL INTO TWO MAIN CATEGORIES. SOME ARE DEVISED FOR A SINGLE PLAYER, THE AIM GENERALLY BEING TO SORT CARDS INTO SUIT SEQUENCES ON A LAYOUT OR TABLEAU. IN COMPETITIVE PATIENCE, SEVERAL PLAYERS COMPETE TO BE THE FIRST TO COMPLETE A GAME. SPECIFIC RULES GOVERN HOW THE CARDS CAN BE ARRANGED AND REARRANGED. THESE SOLITARY GAMES ARE ESPECIALLY SUITABLE FOR PLAY AGAINST A COMPUTER.

Since the first Patience games were devised in the mid-19th century, they have mushroomed. When Britain's Lady Cadogan produced her *Illustrated Games of Patience* in 1874, she was able to list only 24 of them. In contrast, what is generally regarded as today's standard reference, David Parlett's *Penguin Book of Patience*, covers over 250 forms (500, with variations). Even that is not the end of the story. The *Solitaire Central Rulebook* on the Internet currently offers 1,713 different games, and although the list includes some duplication, its compilers conservatively estimate there to be around 1,500 different types of patience.

The aim of the game is to change the position of the cards by 'building' – that is, transferring cards around the tableau. Some can be played immediately, others not until certain blocking cards have been removed. In most games, play starts by placing the cards known as 'foundations', generally the four Aces, into position. After this, the aim is to build on each foundation in sequence and in suit from the Ace through to the King. The gap that is created by moving cards is called a 'space' and knowing how to take advantage of this is a major factor in manipulating the tableau to best advantage. If a player is successful in building the entire pack on to the foundations, the patience 'comes out' and the game is won. If it becomes impossible to sort the cards further, the game is lost and must be abandoned.

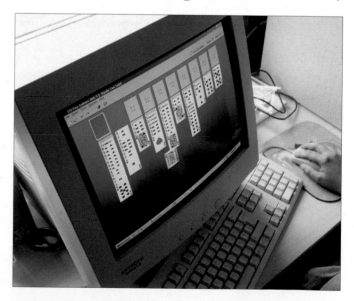

Above: Solitaire is particularly suitable for play against a computer. Many software Solitaire programs can be downloaded from the Internet at no charge.

KLONDIKE

This is probably the best-known game of its ilk in the world, so much so, that many people simply call it Patience or Solitaire without realizing that it has its own name.

You will need:	52-card deck; no Jokers
Card ranking:	None
Players:	One
Ideal for:	4+

OBJECT

To build all four 'suit stacks' from Ace to King.

THE DEAL

Deal seven cards in a row, left to right, upturning the first card. Beginning one place along each time, deal another row, again exposing the first card, until you end up with a 'tableau' (see below) of seven columns, the first comprising a single card, the second two, the third three and so on up to seven. Each column should end with an upturned card. The remaining cards are left face down to form the 'stock pile'.

PLAY

Three cards are turned face up from the stock, but only the top one can be played. If this can be used, the second of the three cards becomes available for play, and so again with the final one. Any exposed Aces from the tableau or at the top of the three cards are removed and placed above the tableau to form the foundation of a suit stack.

Cards that are within the tableau may be built down numerically, although they must alternate in colour – a black Five may be played on a red Six, for instance – while a sequence of cards can be moved in its entirety from one pile to another. Each time a face-up card (or sequence) is moved, the next face-down card is turned over and becomes available for play, with the proviso that in the event an empty space is created on the tableau, only a King can fill it. Exposed cards can be laid in sequence on top of a stacked Ace provided that they are of the same suit.

When all options have been exhausted, any card or cards remaining from the three taken from the stock are placed face up on a 'waste pile' and another three cards turned up, this process being repeated until the stock is exhausted. At any point, the lowest exposed card in a column can be played onto the foundations, or another pile. If the stock becomes exhausted, the waste pile can replace it, but this can happen only twice.

CONCLUSION

The game ends when either all the suits are stacked – the chances of this happening are 1 in 30 – or when no more moves are possible.

Below: In the layout shown, the A♠ should be moved above the tableau to begin a suit stack, with the 2♠ placed on top of it. The card that was under the 2♠ is then turned face upwards. The 9♠ is placed on the 10♦. The card under the 9♠ is then turned face upwards.

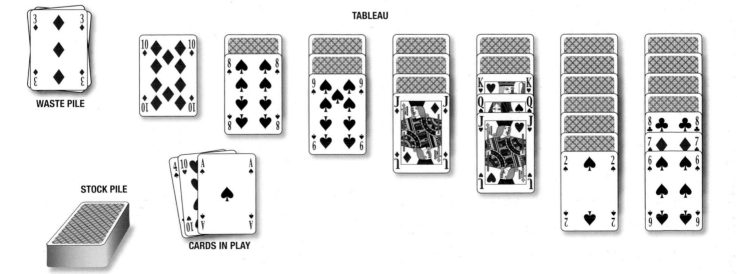

WASTE PILE TABLEAU STOCK PILE CARDS IN PLAY

ACCORDION

It requires persistence to play Accordion successfully, as it takes quite a few deals for the game to come out.

OBJECT

To finish with all the cards in one pile.

THE DEAL

Unlike other games of this genre, there is no tableau – the player simply deals cards singly face up to form a long line from left to right. There is no maximum or minimum number, but experts favour dealing no more than 13 cards at a time.

You will need: 52 cards; no Jokers
Card ranking: None
Players: One
Ideal for: 7+

Below: The cards have been dealt in a line from left to right. The repositioned cards, after the moves (King on King, Heart on Heart etc.) have been taken, are shown underneath.

PLAY

Whenever a card matches the suit or rank of the card immediately to the left of it, it is put on top of the card it matches. This is termed 'packing', after which all the cards to the right are squeezed up to close the gap. Cards can also be moved three places to the left. Packing continues until there is nothing left to pack, at which point more cards are dealt on to the end of the line. Multiple cards must be moved as a complete pile, since matching is limited to the top card. A pile may never be split or separated.

CONCLUSION

The game is won if all the cards can be reduced to a single stack. If not, shuffle the cards and try again.

ACES UP

Somewhat unfairly also known as Idiot's Delight, this is a fast-moving game that requires more skill to play than may be apparent at first glance.

OBJECT

To end up with all four Aces face up in a row and all the other cards discarded in the waste pile.

You will need: 52 cards; no Jokers
Card ranking: None
Players: One
Ideal for: 10+

Below: On the left are the four cards dealt at the start of the game. On the right are the two cards left after the lowest two Diamonds have been discarded.

THE DEAL, PLAY AND CONCLUSION

Four cards are dealt face up in a row. Any card of lower rank and the same suit of another top card can be removed from play. Aces are the highest rank. When all possible cards have been removed, four more cards are then dealt, on top of the remaining ones or on any spaces created. The process continues until all the top cards are of different suits. Four more cards are then dealt on top of these.

If one of the four piles becomes empty, the player can move any top card from any of the other piles into the empty space to create more possible plays. The objective is to remove all cards except for the Aces. The exposed cards precipitate the removal of others as play progresses. The only way to get at cards beneath an Ace is to move the Ace to an empty pile.

Aces Up is easy to play, but it is not easy to win. It all comes down to deciding which card to play into an empty space. To win, you need to end up with just the four Aces face up. If there are any other cards left on the table once the last set of four has been dealt, the game is lost.

LABYRINTH

This is an unusual game in that players are allowed to take the top card of each column as well as the bottom for building on the Ace piles. There may be many gaps in the tableau, giving it the appearance of a labyrinth, as spaces are not filled, except in the first row.

OBJECT

The aim of this game is to build each Ace up into a pile of 13 cards that are arranged in ascending rank order and all in the same suit.

THE DEAL

The four Aces are laid out face up in a row at the top of the table. The rest of the pack is then shuffled and a row of eight cards is dealt face up just below the Aces. Further rows are dealt out during the course of the game.

PLAY

All the cards in the first row are available to start building on the Aces, with new cards being dealt to replace them as needed. When as many cards as possible have been played and any spaces filled, another row of eight cards is dealt. Play proceeds as before, but with one important exception: it is against the rules of the game to fill any more spaces. Instead, once play can go no further, a new row of eight cards must be dealt across the columns underneath the previous row before any further building can take place. All deals must be made in the same direction, usually from left to right.

The last row may consist of fewer than eight cards if cards were used to fill the first row. Strictly speaking this row should be dealt, as far as it can go, in the same direction, but many players prefer to choose which columns to deal the cards to in order to increase the chances of getting the game to come out.

Only the cards in the bottom and top rows are strictly playable. If one can be played from the top row of cards, the card in the bottom row can be played and so on.

You will need: 52-card deck; no Jokers

Card ranking: None, but they are stacked in ascending order

Players: One

Ideal for: 10+

CONCLUSION

The game ends when the stock has been exhausted and every possible move made. If each stack is complete up to Kings, the player has won. If not, better luck next time.

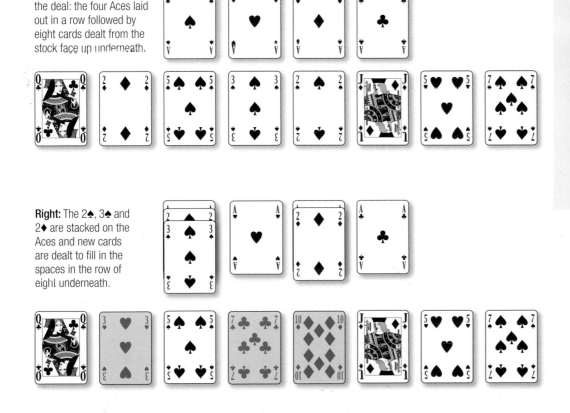

Right: The scenario after the deal: the four Aces laid out in a row followed by eight cards dealt from the stock face up underneath.

Right: The 2♠, 3♠ and 2♦ are stacked on the Aces and new cards are dealt to fill in the spaces in the row of eight underneath.

SPITE AND MALICE

This is a competitive Patience game, sometimes known as Cat and Mouse. It is a variation of the late 19th-century Continental game known as Crapette, Cripette, Robuse and Rabouge.

OBJECT

To be the first to get rid of what is termed a 'riddance pile' of 26 cards by playing them to eight piles that are gradually built up in the centre of the table, starting with an Ace and ending with a King. Suits are irrelevant.

THE DEAL

After it has been shuffled thoroughly, each player receives 26 cards from the 52-card pack without Jokers. These are placed face down to form a riddance pile, and the top card (the 'up-card') of each is turned face up. Both players are then dealt five cards from the second 56-card pack (with Jokers), the remainder forming the stock to be used during the course of play and placed face down between the two players. Jokers can represent any card.

PLAY

A turn consists of a choice of moves. If the up-card is an Ace, the card must be played to start a centre pile. If it is any Two and an Ace has been played, it must be played to that Ace. Playing to a centre pile entitles you to

PLAYER B

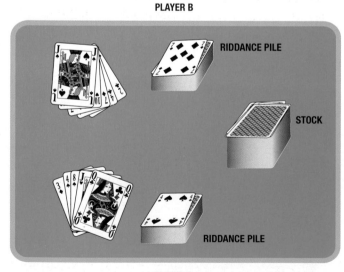

PLAYER A

Above: The scenario at the beginning of Spite and Malice. Both players have 26 cards in their riddance piles, the top card turned up, plus five cards in their hands. The remaining stock pile is placed between the two players.

You will need: Two 52-card decks – one without Jokers and another with four Jokers added as wild cards

Card ranking: None, but cards must be stacked in succession; e.g. Two on Ace, Three on Two

Players: Two

Ideal for: 10+

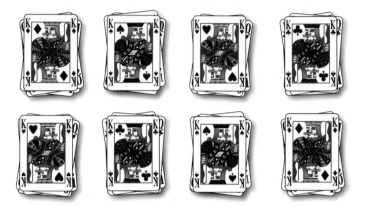

Above: Success – the eight piles from Ace to King are complete. In the game, each stack is turned face down after it is finished.

another turn. So does playing off all five cards in one's hand, after which you draw five more from the stock pile. Cards in a riddance pile can be played only to one of the centre piles. Once a pile is completed (i.e. up to King), it is turned face down and set aside.

The alternative to playing to the centre is to play any card from your hand to a discard pile, except an Ace, replacing it with a card from the stock pile. Up to four such piles may be started by the same player, otherwise players may add to the top of an existing discard pile, if the rank of the discard matches or is one below that of the current top card. The top discard can be played off at any time to a centre pile. If a player cannot make a move, the opposing player plays alone until such time as the frozen player can play again. If both players freeze, all the cards in play except for those in the riddance piles are shuffled and redealt.

SCORING AND CONCLUSION

The winner scores five points, plus a point for every card the loser has not played from his riddance pile.

When the stock is down to 12 cards, all the completed centre piles are combined with it to form a new one. Play continues until one player succeeds in playing off the last card from his riddance pile.

SPIT

Also known as Speed, there are no turns in this game – opponents play simultaneously. This puts a premium on physical speed and mental agility, both of which are essential if one player is to succeed in playing faster than the other.

OBJECT

The object of the game is to get rid of all your cards faster than your opponent.

THE DEAL

Deal 26 cards to two players from a well-shuffled 52-card pack. Each player deals a layout of five stock piles arranged in a row. The first contains a single card, the second two cards and so on up to five.

All the cards are dealt face down, and the top card of each pile is then turned face up. The 11 remaining cards are the 'spit' cards. These must not be examined before they are played.

You will need: 52 cards
Card ranking: None, but cards can only be played to piles in a certain order (see below)
Players: Two
Ideal for: 10+

PLAY

Both players call 'Spit' while turning over the first spit card in their hands. The two cards are placed side-by-side between the players' respective stock piles to form two spit piles. Players now play simultaneously as fast as they can. They can play the turn-up from any of the stock piles on to either spit pile, provided that the card being played is one rank higher or lower than the turn-up. Suits are irrelevant. Alternatively, if one or more of the stock piles have their top cards face down, these can be turned up, while a turn-up can be moved into an empty stock pile space.

A card counts as played as soon as it touches a pile or space. The opposing player can play on it immediately. If neither player can play, both spit again, turn up the next spit card and place it on top of the particular spit pile they started. Play then continues as before. If neither can play and one player has run out of spit cards, the other spits alone on to either pile.

If one player gets rid of all the stock cards or both of them run out of spit cards, a new layout is dealt. Both players choose a spit pile, ideally the smaller one, by slapping it with their hands. If both choose the same one, the player hitting it first has preference.

Both players then add any remaining spit or stock cards to their respective piles, shuffle their cards and deal new layouts. When the players are ready, they call 'Spit' and play again. If one of the players has fewer than 15 cards, he should deal them into five piles as far as he can and turn each top card over. As this player is unable to spit, there will be only one spit pile, started by the other player.

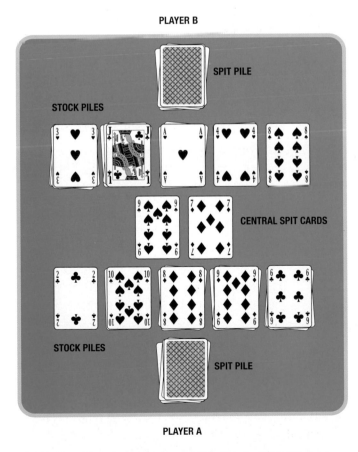

PLAYER B

SPIT PILE

STOCK PILES

CENTRAL SPIT CARDS

STOCK PILES

SPIT PILE

PLAYER A

Above: Player A can play the 8♦, 9♦ and 10♠ on to the 7♦, but he needs to be quick, as Player B might try to play the 8♠ on to the 7♦.

CONCLUSION

When one spit pile remains and a player runs out of stock cards, the other plays on until he gets stuck. He collects all the cards from the table, deals and spits again. The first to run out of stock and spit cards wins.

Nerts

Also known as Pounce, Racing Demon, Peanuts and Squeal, this is a competitive Patience game that can be played by more than two players if you have enough packs of cards.

You will need: Two (or more) different 52-card packs; no Jokers
Card ranking: None, but piles must be built in order
Players: Two (or more)
Ideal for: 7+

Object

To be the first player to play all the cards in his 'nerts' pile on to four foundation piles.

The Deal

Each player plays with his own pack. Both players deal a nerts pile, 12 cards face down and the last face up, with four more placed face up to form a row of work piles. The remaining cards are kept face down as a stock.

Play

Players use the work piles to sort their cards. They are built in descending order and alternating in colour so, for example, a red Six would be placed on a black Seven. The lowest-ranked cards are available to be played on to the foundations. Players may transfer any card from one work pile to another, together with all the cards on top of it. Foundation piles, each of which must be started with an Ace, are built upwards in suit and sequence. Any player can play to any pile when they hold the next card

in the sequence. If two players choose the same pile, the fastest one wins and the other player has to take his back. Foundation cards are communal, with all players having access. Cards from nerts piles can be played to empty spaces in work piles, on to existing work piles, or on to foundation piles. As soon as the top card of a nerts pile is played, the next is turned face up. When a player's pile is exhausted, he can call 'Nerts', stopping play. Players, if stuck, are allowed to turn over stock pile cards three at a time and place them in a waste pile, from which the top card can be played. If every player gets stuck, each waste pile is turned to form a new stock, the top card of the stock being transferred to the bottom.

Scoring and Conclusion

One point is scored for each card played to a foundation pile. Two points are deducted for each card left in a player's nerts pile. Deals are played up to an agreed target.

PLAYER B

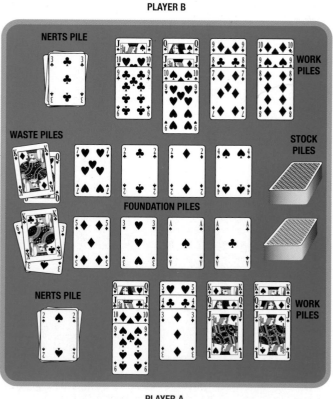

PLAYER A

PLAYER B

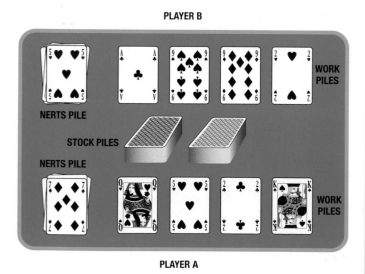

PLAYER A

Above: Each player has a nerts pile. The top card is face up and there are four face-up cards that form the work piles.

Right: Player A can play the 2♠ from his nerts pile on to the Ace in his foundation pile and the 3♦ from his work pile on to his opponent's foundation pile. Player B can also play the 3♣ from his nerts pile on to his foundation pile.

POKER PATIENCE

Also known as Poker Solitaire and Poker Squares, this game is unusual because only 25 cards are actively employed. Unlike most solitaire games, where the aim is to put cards into a preset order, the aim here is to put the cards into certain combinations that correspond to standard Poker hands.

You will need: 52 cards; no Jokers

Card ranking: See 'Scoring and Ranking', below

Players: One (or can be played competitively)

Ideal for: 14+

OBJECT

To move cards one at a time out of the stock pile and position them anywhere on a 'grid' of five cards by five cards, so that each of the latter's rows and columns forms the best possible Poker hand ranking. The better the hands that can be created, the higher the score. To win the game, a player needs to score at least 200 points in the American system or 70 points in the English one. The game can be played competitively, in which case the highest score wins.

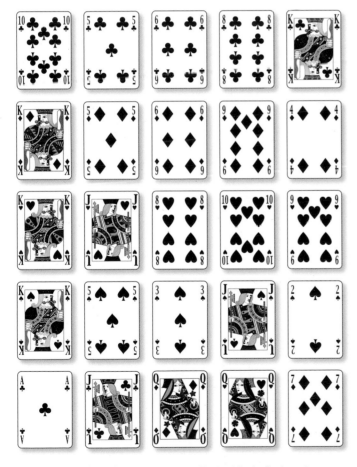

Above: The first four rows here all show a Flush while the final row has a Pair (of Queens). The first column has Three of a Kind (Kings), the second a Full House, the third a Pair (two Sixes), and the fourth a Straight.

THE DEAL

The player shuffles the pack and deals the first 25 cards face up into a pile to become the stock for the first grid. The remaining cards are kept in reserve for a second one.

PLAY

A typical strategy is to try to establish Flushes on the first four rows and Full Houses, Fours of a Kind, or Straights on the columns. The last row is often used as a dumping ground for cards that do not fit elsewhere in the layout.

Straights are high scoring but are the hardest to create. The alternative is to settle for lower-scoring, but safer, hands, such as Pairs and Three of a Kind. Even the best plans can be spoilt by bad luck. Once a card has been placed, it cannot be moved, nor may the next card in the stock be examined until the turn-up is placed.

SCORING AND RANKING

There are two scoring systems – American and English (given in brackets). Cards are also ranked as follows:

- 100 (30) points for a Royal Flush: A Straight Flush (see below) up to Ace.
- 75 (30) for a Straight Flush: Five cards in sequence and of the same suit.
- 50 (18) for Four of a Kind: Four cards of the same face value.
- 25 (10) for a Full House: Three of a Kind and a Pair.
- 20 (five) for a Flush: Five cards of the same suit.
- 15 (12) for a Straight: A sequence of five cards in any suit.
- 10 (6) for Three of a Kind: Three cards of the same face value.
- 5 (3) for Two Pairs of the same face value.
- 2 (1) for One Pair of the same face value.

CONCLUSION

The game is finished when all the cards have been laid out on to the grid.

2 | POINT-TRICK GAMES

WINNING AND LOSING POINT-TRICK GAMES DEPENDS ON THE POINT VALUES OF INDIVIDUAL CARDS TAKEN WITHIN TRICKS AND NOT ON THE ACTUAL NUMBER OF TRICKS WON OR LOST. A TRICK IS A ROUND OF CARDS, WHERE ONE CARD IS PLAYED BY EACH PLAYER IN THE GAME. A TRICK IS WON WITH THE HIGHEST CARD OF THE SUIT LED OR BY THE HIGHEST TRUMP. MANY GAMES INCLUDE BIDDING, IN WHICH SOME BIDS HAVE AIMS SUCH AS LOSING ALL THE TRICKS.

The games range from France's Manille, which originated as Malilla in Spain, to Stovkahra, the only surviving descendant of a strange Italian game called Trappola, first played in Venice in 1524. Stovkahra is a rare Romanian game, in which the aim is to be the first partnership to win 100 points. On its home turf, it is played with a 32-card German-suited pack (the German suits of Acorns, Leaves, Hearts and Bells correspond to Clubs, Spades, Hearts and Diamonds, repectively). Players score by declaring card combinations, such as Three or Four of a Kind, other than Eights and Nines, taking card points in tricks and winning any trick with a Seven. Winning the first and the last trick with a Seven is worth bonus points – 52 points and 26 points, respectively.

Point-trick games have not just been confined to the West, and many games not mentioned in this book are popular in the East. In Japan, Etoni, or 'capturing pictures', originated in the early 1900s, while Napoleon (not the British game of the same name) is one of the country's most popular games. Mighty, played mostly in Korea, is a related game in which Aces, Kings, Queens, Jacks and frequently Tens are worth a point each. The A♠, which is known in Japanese as *ohrumaita* or simply *maita* ('almighty' or 'mighty'), enjoys a special status. It can beat any other card, including trumps.

Above: Japanese women playing cards (*c.*1867). The concept of card games was introduced in Japan as early as the 16th century by Portugese traders.

MANILLE

There are a number of versions of this partnership game, of which the most popular are Manille Muette, which is played in silence; Manille Parlée, in which partners are permitted to share a single piece of information about their cards, or suggest what card or suit to lead; and Manille à l'Envers (Reverse Manille). Manille was France's national card game from around 1870 until the end of the Second World War, when Belote finally eclipsed it in popularity.

OBJECT

The aim is to be the first to win two successive deals, or to secure an agreed number of points.

THE DEAL

Each player is dealt eight cards, four at a time, with the dealer turning his last card up to establish the trump suit – that is, the suit of cards that outranks all others – laying it on the table until the first card is led.

PLAY

The player to the dealer's left leads to the first trick. Players have to follow suit if they can; if not, they can play a trump. The highest card of the suit led takes the trick, or the highest trump, if trumps are played. If a player's partner is winning a trick, that player is not obliged to follow suit or trump. If an opponent is winning, however, suit must be followed or a trump played. The highest card of the suit led or the highest trump takes the trick and the winner leads to the next.

SCORING

Each trick taken is worth a point. Five extra points are scored for a trick containing a Ten (*Manille*), four for an Ace (*Manillon*), three for a King, two for a Queen and one for a Jack. If a trick contains more than one of these, points are scored for each.

CONCLUSION

To win a hand, a partnership needs to score a minimum of 35 points. Convention has it that the target score for game is either 100 or 200 points.

You will need: 52 cards; no Jokers

Card ranking: The Ten ranks highest, followed by Ace, King, Queen, Jack and Nine to Two

Players: Four

Ideal for: 10ı

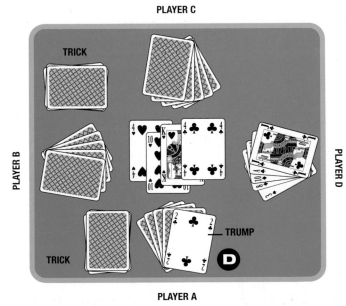

PLAYER C

PLAYER B

PLAYER D

PLAYER A

Above: Player D discards, as his partner is winning the trick with the 10♣. He could have followed suit with the A♣ or J♣, or played a trump with the Q♥, but since his partner is winning, he can hold on to his better cards.

PLAYER C

PLAYER B

PLAYER D

PLAYER A

Above: Unable to follow suit in this trick, Player D has played the trump (4♣), thus winning it. Player D's partnership scores an extra three points for the King and an extra five for the Ten.

SPANISH SOLO

Widely popular in South America and Spain, this game is a cross between Tresillo, the modern form of Ombre, and Manille. Unlike the latter, it includes bidding. Each player puts one of their chips into the pool before starting. When playing with children, use counters or candies.

You will need: 36-card pack, Tens, Nines, Eights and Twos having been removed; gambling chips/counters

Card ranking: Seven is highest, then Ace, King, Queen, etc.

Players: Three

Ideal for: 14+

OBJECT

The aim of the game is to fulfil a specified contract and/or score the most points in a hand.

THE DEAL

Each player is dealt 12 cards, four at a time.

BIDDING

There are three bids, which rank in the following order:

- *Juego* (Solo) – a bid to win at least 37 points (36 points if the bidder is the player to the dealer's left). It is worth two game points or four in Diamonds.
- *Bola* (Slam) – a bid to win every trick, having named wanted card and exchanged an unwanted one for it. Its value is eight game points, 12 in Diamonds.
- *Bola sin Pedir* (No-call Slam) – the highest bid, contracting to take every trick without exchanging a card. Its value is 16 points, or 20 in Diamonds.

THE AUCTION

Starting with the player to the dealer's left, each player in turn must either bid or pass. If the former, the bid must be higher than the one preceding it. If a player passes, he puts another chip into the pool and sits out the rest of the auction. The successful bidder becomes the soloist and announces trumps. If these are Diamonds, the value of the bid increases, as shown above. If everyone passes, it is down to the dealer to choose trumps. The hand is still played.

PLAY

The player to the dealer's right leads. The other players must follow suit if possible. Otherwise, they may play a trump or, failing that, any card. The highest card of the suit led wins the trick, or the highest trump if any are played. The most valuable cards in each suit are the Seven (*Malilla*), followed by the Ace, King, Queen and Jack. The soloist now tries to fulfil the bid and other players try to score as many points as they can.

SCORING

- Five points for a trick containing a Seven.
- Four points for a trick containing an Ace.
- Three points for a trick containing a King.
- Two points for a trick containing a Queen.
- One point for a trick containing a Jack.

The winner of each trick scores an extra point.

CONCLUSION

The player scoring the most card points wins the hand. He then receives two chips from the player with the fewest number of points and one chip from the player with the second lowest score. If a soloist's contract is successful, he receives the appropriate number of chips from each opponent, two chips for a successful *Juego*, for instance, and wins the pool. If not, he pays the value of the failed bid to the opposing players and doubles what is in the pool.

Left: With a long strong suit in Diamonds, the natural bid for this player is *Juego* (Solo), naming Diamonds as trumps.

FIFTEENS

This old German game is straightforward to play, but has a twist in its tail concerning the cards that can be led.

OBJECT
To win as many points as possible and end the game with the most chips.

THE DEAL
Players are dealt eight cards each face down.

PLAY
The player to the left of dealer leads to the first trick, and the highest card played wins. The winner of that first trick must lead the same suit to the next, playing his highest card. The next person to win the lead does the same. If he holds no cards of that suit, he must revert to the suit played to take the previous trick or, if still void, the one before that. The next to play also does the same.

You will need: 32-card pack with those below Seven removed; no Jokers; gambling chips/counters

Card ranking: Standard

Players: Four

Ideal for: 10+

A King and Queen of the same suit in a hand is known as a *Zwang* (force). A player holding one declares it upon leading the Queen. This forces the holder of the Ace to play it, leaving the King high. Otherwise, the Ace's holder is free to underplay in the hope of winning the King later.

SCORING AND CONCLUSION
Aces score five, Kings four, Queens three, Jacks two and Tens one. Each player calculates the value of the cards taken in tricks and pays a chip to the pot for every point he is short of 15, or wins a chip for every point that exceeds 15. Players settle up chips at the end of the game.

FORTY FOR KINGS

This 18th-century partnership game was played in France and Germany, where it was known as Quarante de Roi and Vierzig von König respectively.

OBJECT
The aim is to score points for *Cliques* (three or four court cards of the same rank) and for tricks (a round of cards) containing court cards (Kings, Queens, Jacks).

THE DEAL
Players are dealt eight cards in packets of three, two and three face down.

PLAY
The dealer shows his last card to set trumps. Each player then announces and scores for any *Cliques* held. The player to the left of the dealer leads. Players must follow suit or otherwise play any card. The highest card of the led suit or the highest trump takes the trick. The winner leads to the next. Each partnership scores for all the court cards it captures, adding this to its score for *Cliques*.

You will need: 32-card pack, the lowest card is Seven

Card ranking: King, Queen, Jack, Ace, Ten, Nine, Eight, Seven

Players: Four, in partnerships of two

Ideal for: 10+

SCORING AND CONCLUSION
Four Kings score 40 and three score 10, while Queens score 20 and eight, and Jacks score 13 and six. The court cards are worth five, four and three points each when they are captured in tricks. At the end of a trick, the partnerships score all the court cards they have taken and add the total to their scores for *Cliques*. Game is 150 points.

A running total of points is kept, and the first partnership with 150 points (or an agreed amount) wins.

Left: A *Clique* of three Kings is 10 points in Forty for Kings.

TRESSETTE

One of Italy's most popular card games, Tressette, unlike most positive point-trick games, is played without trumps. It is characterized by a distinctive signalling system between partners.

OBJECT

To score as many points in each hand as possible, until you have reached the winning total, usually 21.

THE DEAL

Each player is dealt 10 cards face down, five at a time.

SIGNALLING

When leading to a trick, three verbal or physical signals are allowed. A call of 'Busso' is a signal to the caller's partner to play the highest card of the suit that has been led, the sign being to tap the card or the table with a fist. Saying 'Volo' means that the caller has no more cards of the suit led, the sign being to glide the card slowly across the table. 'Striscio' means that the lead is the caller's strongest suit, in which case the sign is to flick the card quickly on to the table.

PLAY

The player to the left of the dealer leads. Players must follow suit or otherwise play any card. There are no trumps. The highest-ranking card of the suit led wins the trick, the winner leading to the next trick. The cards rank and count in descending order from Three, Two, Ace, King, Queen and Jack to Seven, Six, Five and Four.

SCORING

Only Aces and court cards have individual point values, but certain card combinations also score. Each Ace is worth a point and each Three, Two or court card scores one-third of a point. The winner of the last trick gets a further point. Any fractions in the end totals are ignored. Scores are rounded down to the nearest whole number.

Certain card combinations must be declared and scored at the end of the first trick. A player holding four Aces, Threes or Twos (Four of a Kind) scores four points, and holding three (Three of a Kind) scores three. A *Napoletana*, when a player holds a Three, Two and Ace of the same suit, is three points. When declaring a *Napoletana*, its suit must be specified. So, too, must the

You will need: 40-card deck (Eights, Nines and Tens having been removed from a standard pack)

Card ranking: Three, Two, Ace, King, Queen, Jack, Seven, Six, Five, Four

Players: The standard version is a game for four, playing in partnerships of two, but it can be played by up to eight players

Ideal for: 14+

missing suit be specified when declaring Three of a Kind, otherwise it is invalid. There are several ways to win more points. When a partnership takes all 10 tricks, the points are doubled. This is termed *Cappotto*. When a partership wins all the points, but not all the tricks, the points are trebled (known as *Stramazzo*). *Cappottone*, which occurs when a single player takes all the tricks, wins sixfold. *Strammazzone*, which occurs when one player wins all the points and the opposing partnership wins at least one trick, wins eightfold. *Collatondrione*, which occurs when a single player declares all 10 cards of a suit, wins 16-fold.

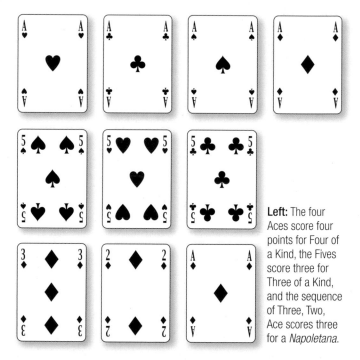

Left: The four Aces score four points for Four of a Kind, the Fives score three for Three of a Kind, and the sequence of Three, Two, Ace scores three for a *Napoletana*.

CONCLUSION

Once all 10 tricks have been played, each partnership scores the value of the cards it has taken in tricks, plus, if applicable, the point for taking the final trick. The partnership that scores 21 points first wins.

TERZIGLIO

Also known as Calabresella, this well-established Italian game is notable, like Tressette, for its unusual card rankings and lack of trumps. Unlike Tressette, there is a round of bidding, and card combinations are ignored and do not score.

OBJECT

The overall aim is to be the first player to reach 21 points by capturing tricks containing valuable cards.

THE DEAL

Each player is dealt 12 cards four at a time. The remaining four cards, the *Monte*, are placed face down on the table.

BIDDING AND EXCHANGING

Starting with the player to the dealer's left, each player bids or passes, and a player who has passed may not come in again. Each successive bid should improve on the last. The bids from low to high are:

- *Chiamo* (Call) – if successful, the bidder is entitled to ask if any of the other players is holding a specific card. If one is, he hands it over, getting a card back from the bidder in exchange. If not, the bidder picks up the *Monte*, discarding four cards face down to form a new one. Whoever wins the last trick will win the *Monte* and benefit from any card-points it may contain.
- *Solo* – same as above, but the bidder does not ask the others for a card.
- *Solissimo* – the player plays with the cards as dealt, does not call a card, takes the *Monte* and discards as above.
- *Solissimo Dividete* – here, the player may choose to increase the stakes by calling 'Dividete' (Half each), whereby the opposing players each take two cards from the *Monte* and discard two.
- *Solissimo Scegliete* – here, by calling 'Scegliete' (You choose), the four cards of the *Monte* are turned face up and the opposing players agree on the split, 2–2, 3–1, or 4–0, each discarding as many as they take accordingly.

PLAY

The player to the dealer's right leads to the first trick, unless *Solissimo* was bid, in which case the bidder leads. Players must follow suit if possible, otherwise they may play any card. There are no trumps. The person to place

the highest card of the suit led wins the trick. The winner of each trick leads to the next one. To win the hand, the bidder must score at least six points, in which case each opponent loses points, depending on what was bid.

SCORING

Each Ace scores a point and each Three, Two or court card one-third of a point. The winner of the final trick not only scores a point for being last but also wins a bonus point for the *Monte*. This counts as an extra trick. *Chiamo* is worth one point, *Solo* two, *Solissimo* four, *Solissimo Dividete* eight and *Solissimo Scegliete* 16. Should the bid fail, the bidder's opponents score the points. If the bidder wins or loses every trick, the amount won or paid to their opponents is doubled. If he wins or loses all the points, the amount won or paid out is trebled.

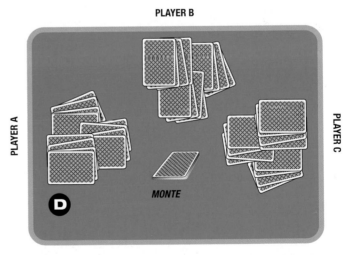

Above: Cards are dealt to each player in three packets of four, the remaining cards forming the *Monte*. Player B will be first to start the bidding, after which Player C leads to the first trick, unless Player B bids *Solissimo*.

CONCLUSION

The game ends when a player scores 21 points, but a target of 31 or 51 may be agreed.

Ciapanò

This intriguing game originated in Milan and is the reverse of Tressette. It is also known as Rovescino, Traversone, Tressette a non Prendere, Perdivinci and Vinciperdi.

Object
To avoid taking any trick containing valuable cards, or winning the final trick, which carries an extra penalty.

The Deal
Each player is dealt the same number of cards – eight if there are five players, 10 for four, and 13 for three. In the last case, the dealer takes 14 cards and discards one, which is given to the winner of the last trick.

Play
The player to the dealer's right leads. Any card may be led, the other players following suit if they can. If not, they can play any card. There are no trumps. The highest card of the suit led takes the trick, the winner leading to the next.

You will need: 40-card deck (Eights, Nines and Tens removed from a standard pack)

Card ranking: Threes rank highest, followed by the Twos, the Aces, the court cards, Sevens, Sixes, Fives and Fours

Players: Three, four or five

Ideal for: 14+

Scoring
In this game, each Ace is worth a point and Threes, Twos and court cards score one-third of a point each. When all the tricks have been played, each player, with the exception of the player who took the final trick, adds up the value of the cards he has taken as penalty points. If there are any fractions left over once the points have been added up, these should be discounted. For instance, a player with three-and-a-third points would score only three points. A player with less than one point would score nothing.

The winner of the last trick scores the total of the other players' scores minus 11. The penalty for winning the last trick varies. It can count for one, two or three points depending on how the other tricks are distributed among the players. If one player wins all the points, this is termed *Cappotto*. He scores zero and the other players score 11 penalty points each. Once a player's cumulative score reaches 31 points or more, he drops out of the game, although by prior agreement this can be raised or lowered by 10 points.

Conclusion
When only two players are left in, the one with the lower score wins.

Left: 18th-century French playing cards. Originating in Milan and played widely in France, Ciapanò is typically played with Italian- or French-suited packs.

Below: The 3♠ and 3♥ are the highest cards in this hand, followed by A♠, K♦, Q♦, J♠, the 7♥ and 7♣, the 6♣ and the 2♥.

DA BAI FEN

Roughly translated, Da Bai Fen means 'competing for 100 points', which is the total number of card points in the pack. In China, where the game was invented, there are other versions.

You will need: 52 cards, with the addition of two Jokers as extra trumps

Card ranking: See 'Trumps and Ranks', below

Players: Four players, in partnership

Ideal for: 14+

OBJECT

To win tricks containing counting cards (Kings, Tens and Fives, worth 10, 10 and five points respectively), and to take the last trick of a hand, until your partnership has won a hand of every trump rank, finishing with Aces.

TRUMPS AND RANKS

There are 18 trumps: the two Jokers, the cards of the suit elected trumps during the deal, plus the other three cards of a particular rank (which at the start of the game is the Two). From highest to lowest, trumps rank as follows: red Joker, black Joker, the card of the trump rank and trump suit (2♠ initially, if Spades are trumps), the other three cards of the trump rank (2♥, 2♣, 2♦) and then the remaining cards of the trump suit from Ace down to Two.

At the start, Two is always the trump rank, so the player who first draws a Two in the deal and his partner become the declarers and play first. The player who drew the Two also has the right to declare its suit as trumps. The two players stay declarers until they lose a hand, when their opponents take over. Afterwards, the declarers' current score determines the trump rank. If, for example, they have 10 game points, the trump rank is Tens, 11 means that it is Jacks, 12 Queens, 13 Kings and 14 Aces.

THE DEAL

Players sit crosswise in agreed partnerships. One player at random is designated the 'starter', who shuffles the cards. They are then cut by either opponent before being placed face down on the table. The starter draws first, followed by the next player to the right and so on around the table. The draw continues until everyone has 12 cards in hand, with six remaining on the table.

Once a trump suit has been declared, the player who declared it picks up the six table cards and discards six cards face down. If no trumps are declared, the six table cards are turned up one at a time. The first card of the trump rank to appear determines the trump suit. If none of the trump rank appear, then the trump suit is the highest of the exposed cards (other than Jokers).

PLAY

In the first hand, the player who declared trumps starts; subsequently, each trick's winner leads. The leader can lead one card or several cards of the same suit with the proviso that the latter must all outrank any cards of the same suit held by the other players. If this is not the case, a 'revoke', or penalty, is declared. This stops play and the offended opposing partnership scores as though it had won every trick.

The other players must play as many cards as were led. Suit must be followed if possible, otherwise trumps may be played. The highest card of the suit led or the highest trump wins. As play progresses, all players extract the Kings, Tens and Fives from the tricks they have won and place them face up on the table. Other cards are put face down into a waste pile.

SCORING AND CONCLUSION

At the end of play, the six discards are turned up and its counting cards scored, along with the counting cards the players have won. The number of card points won by the opposing partnership determines the result. This decides who scores how many game points and who will be the declarers for the next hand.

If the opposers score between zero and five card points, the declarers score two game points. However, if the opposers score between five and 35 card points, the declarers score one game point. If the score is between 40 and 75 card points, no game points are scored. In all three instances, the declarers remain the declarers. If, however, the opposers score between 80 and 95 or more than 100 card points, they win one or two game points and become the declarers.

In each hand, a partnership's score is determined by the trump rank when they become declarers. If, for example, a side with a score of nine gains two game points in a hand, their score goes up to 'Jack'. The first partnership to reach Aces (i.e. 14 game points) and win a hand with Aces as the trump rank, wins the game.

3 | CATCH AND COLLECT GAMES

CATCHING GAMES – CARD GAMES IN WHICH THE OBJECTIVE IS TO CAPTURE ALL THE CARDS – ARE EXTREMELY OLD. ALTHOUGH MANY OF THEM ARE CLASSIC CHILDREN'S GAMES, THIS DOES NOT PRECLUDE THEM FROM BEING GAMES OF SKILL. AS THE NAME IMPLIES, COLLECT GAMES REVOLVE AROUND COLLECTING CARDS. THESE CAN BE PAIRS OF CARDS OF MATCHING RANKS OR SETS OF CARDS THAT ARE MATCHED IN RANK OR BY SUIT.

These types of games can be as simple as Snap (although success here still involves speeds of recognition and reaction), Happy Families (the American version of which is Go Fish) and Authors. The latter is an American game for children, but there is an adult version of the game, called Literature, which is a partnership card game for six or eight players. It revolves around the players questioning their opponents about the cards in their hands and acquiring cards accordingly.

Some more obscure games have their own endearing features. In Pig, players signal the end of a game by touching their noses – the last player to do so is the 'pig' – while in Spoons, they grab for a spoon. Other games, such as Gops or Schwimmen, are more complex. The former is an acronym for 'Game of Pure Strategy', reflecting the tactical skill needed to play the game well. In Schwimmen, the idea is for players to improve their hands in turn by swapping a card at a time for a face-up card on the table. It is particularly popular in Germany and in some parts of Austria.

Whisky Poker was invented in the USA, where it was given its name for fairly self-evident reasons. It was played widely in the late 19th and early 20th centuries, and it still has an American following today. Despite its name and the fact it uses ranking, it is played in an entirely different way to Poker: the chief difference is that no betting is involved.

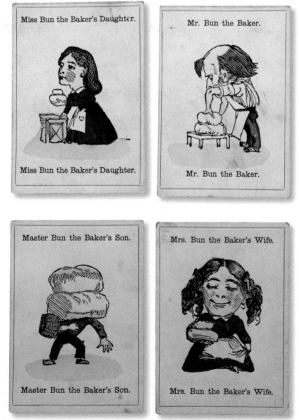

Above: 19th-century playing cards showing the Baker family from the game Happy Families. The aim is to collect families of four.

CARD-CATCHING GAMES

The simplest and possibly best-known game of this type is Snap, followed by Beggar-My-Neighbour, also known as Beat Your Neighbour Out of Doors. Slapjack is a fun game, which revolves around physically slapping a Jack whenever it appears, while Memory is just what its name implies – a real test of card recall.

SNAP

Players hold their cards face down. Each in turn plays their top card face up to the middle of the table as quickly as possible. When the card played matches the rank of the preceding card, the player who calls 'Snap' first wins the central pool of cards. As players run out of cards, they drop out of play.

If someone calls 'Snap' by mistake – or if two or more players call simultaneously – the pool is placed face up to one side and a new one started. When a card played to the new pool matches the top card of the old one, the player to call 'Snap pool' first wins both pools.

BEGGAR-MY-NEIGHBOUR

Players take it in turns to turn over their top cards and place them face up in the middle of the table. There are two types of card: Ace, King, Queen and Jack are paying cards and the others are ordinary ones.

When a player places a pay card, the opponent has to place four cards for an Ace, three for a King, two for a Queen and one for a Jack. If these cards are all ordinary, the player of the pay card scoops the pool. But if the opponent plays a pay card, the reverse applies. The player who runs out of cards first loses.

Above: Memory involves turning up two pairs from cards scattered face down on the table. Whether through good luck or memory, this player turns up a matching pair, and so keeps the cards.

SLAPJACK

Players hold their cards as face-down piles, each in turn playing the top card face up to the centre of the table. When a Jack is played, the first player to slap it wins the central pile. The winner is the player ending up with all the cards.

In another version, the aim is to lose cards, not win them. Players try to predict what card they are playing by calling out a rank. If card and call match, all the players race to slap the pile. The last one to do so adds the pile to the cards he is holding.

MEMORY

The cards are dealt at random face down over the table, after which each player in turn picks up and announces two of them. If the cards form a pair, that player wins them and has another go; if not, they are replaced face down in the same position and it is the next player's turn. The player with the sharpest memory normally wins.

PLAYER B

PLAYER A

Left: In this example of Beggar-My-Neighbour, Player A has laid a Jack, and so does not have to place four cards. This means that Player B has to place one new pay card.

Gops

This strange game is a test of strategy – its name is an acronym of the term Game of Pure Strategy. It is very popular among game theorists as it is susceptible to logical mathematical analysis. It is also known as Goofspiel.

Object

To win the greatest value of Diamonds, or whichever is the chosen suit, until reaching the required point total.

The Deal

The pack is split into its suits, with one – usually Diamonds – being singled out as the so-called competition suit. The remaining suits are divided between the players. If only two are playing, one suit is discarded. The competition suit is shuffled and placed face down on the table, to form the competition stack.

Play and Scoring

Play begins with the top card of the competition suit being turned face up. Players then bid for the card in turn by choosing any card from their hands and placing it face down on the table. When all the cards have been placed, they are turned over. Whichever player has played the highest one wins the competition card. The bid cards, as they are termed, are put aside and the next turn is played.

You will need: 52 cards for three players, but with one suit taken out when there are two players

Card ranking: Standard, Aces low

Players: Two to three

Ideal for: 14+

In the event of a tie between the bidders in a two- or three-player game, the competition card is either discarded or rolled over to the next round, to be taken by the next competition card winner. If there are three players and two tie for best bid, the card goes to the third player.

Gops is difficult to master, since it presents its players with a series of dilemmas that have to be resolved. The skill comes from gauging correctly when to bid high for a card and when to bid low, forcing the opposing players to bid more than they need to take a certain card.

Aces count as one, numbered cards at their face values, Jack 11, Queen 12 and King 13.

Conclusion

The game is over once all 13 cards from the competition stack have been taken. In a two-player game, the player scoring 46 points or more wins; in the three-player version, the target score is 31 points.

Above: After the deal, the top card of the competition stack is turned over. Players then bid on it by placing one card face down in front of them.

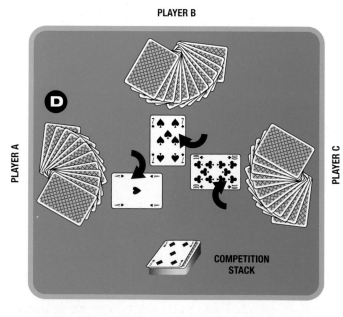

Above: After the deal, all players turn over their bid cards at the same time, and Player C's 10♣ wins over the 5♦.

SCHWIMMEN

Known in English-speaking countries as Thirty-One, Schwimmen is also called Schnautz, Knack and Hosen'runter in Germany and western Austria. Players improve their hands by exchanging cards into a central pool of turned-up cards.

OBJECT

To score nearest to 31 or 32 points by collecting cards of the same suit or holding three cards of the same rank.

THE DEAL

Each player receives an equal number of chips and then is dealt three cards face down, with an extra three being dealt on to the table. The dealer decides whether to play with his dealt hand or exchange it sight unseen with the spare one. The rejected cards are then turned face up.

PLAY

The player to the left of the dealer plays first, the turn to play passing clockwise around the table. Each player is entitled to exchange a card for one of the cards face up on the table, or pass.

Above: After the cards are dealt, each player has the opportunity to exchange one of his cards with the cards face up on the table. Here, the four players have passed, so the face-up cards are replaced by three new ones.

> **You will need:** 32-card pack created by removing the cards from Two to Six; gambling chips/counters
>
> **Card ranking:** See 'Scoring and Conclusion', below
>
> **Players:** Two to eight
>
> **Ideal for:** 10+

Above: The game ends if a *Feuer* (three Aces) is declared by a player.

If all of the players pass in succession, the face-up cards are then replaced with new ones from the stock pile, and the game continues.

Any player can decide to 'close' at the end of his turn, after which the others have one more chance to play before the hand is over. The hand also ends if certain sets of cards are disclosed. There are two of these: *Feuer* (fire), comprising three Aces (32 points), and *Schnautz*, featuring three cards of the same suit, worth 31 points. Both of them must be declared as soon as they are made.

To score, all player's cards are exposed and the values of cards in any one suit calculated. If play ends because a player closes or declares *Schnautz*, the player with the worst hand loses a chip. If *Feuer* is declared, all the players except the declarer lose a chip. Once a player has lost all his chips, he is said to be 'swimming'. Although he can continue to play, he may do so only until he loses another hand, when he must drop out of the game.

SCORING AND CONCLUSION

Aces are worth 11 points and the court cards 10 each, while the numbered cards count at face value. Only cards of the same suit are scored. Thus, a hand containing the K♣, 7♥ and 9♥ is worth 16 points for the two Hearts – the King does not score. Three cards of the same rank (Three of a Kind) other than Aces score 30.5 points. If scores are tied, a higher Three of a Kind beats a lower one, as does a higher suit, ranked Clubs, Spades, Hearts and Diamonds. The last player in the game is the winner.

WHISKY POKER

In this one-time American favourite, players have the chance to improve their hands by exchanging cards with a spare hand, known as the widow, which is dealt to the table.

You will need: 52 cards, no wild cards; gambling chips/counters

Card ranking: Standard. Hands are also ranked (see below)

Players: Two to nine players

Ideal for: 14+

OBJECT

To collect the best five-card poker hand, the player with the highest hand scooping the pool.

THE DEAL

Before choosing the dealer for each round, every player puts a chip into a communal pot. They draw to decide who deals first, the player with the lowest card having the honour. Five cards are dealt to each player, starting with the player to the dealer's left, with the widow being dealt immediately before the dealer's own hand. The widow is kept face down in the centre of the table. After the first hand, the deal passes to the left around the table.

PLAY

The player to the dealer's left starts by deciding whether to exchange his hand as dealt for the widow. If not, the next player is given the same opportunity and so on round the table. If no one exchanges, the widow is turned face up and play begins.

Each player in turn now has one of three options. He can exchange one card (discarding a card face up and taking a replacement from the widow), exchange all five cards, or knock, signalling the imminent ending of play. The other players have one more turn, after which there is a showdown with the best hand winning the pot.

SCORING AND RANKING

From lowest to highest, the ranking of hands are:

- High card – a hand with no combinations, but with the highest-ranking card among the hands in play.
- One Pair – two cards of the same value; e.g. 3♦, 3♥ or Q♠, Q♣. If another player holds a Pair of the same value, then whoever holds the highest card in the two hands (called the 'kicker'), wins.
- Two Pairs – two sets of Pairs; e.g. 3♦, 3♥ and Q♠, Q♣. Again, whoever holds the 'kicker' wins if two players hold matching Pairs of the same value.
- Three of a Kind – three cards of the same face value (this is also known as 'trips'); e.g. Q♠, Q♣, Q♥.
- Straight – a sequence of five cards in any suit; e.g. 5♦, 6♣, 7♠, 8♥, 9♣. The highest Straight is one topped by Ace, the lowest starts with Ace. Should two players hold a Straight the one with the highest cards wins.
- Flush – five cards of the same suit. If another player holds a Flush, whoever holds the highest card wins.
- Full House – Three of a Kind and a Pair. When two players hold a Full House, the one with the highest ranking trips wins.
- Four of a Kind – four cards of the same face value (known as 'quads').
- Straight Flush – a combined Straight and Flush, which contains cards in sequence and of same suit.
- Royal Flush – a Straight Flush up to Ace.

The player with the highest-ranking hand takes the pot of chips. Alternatively, each player can start with five chips and the player with the weakest hand forfeits one of these, the first to lose all five chips becomes the overall loser.

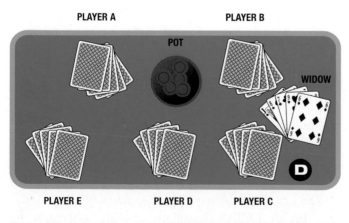

PLAYER A   POT   PLAYER B

WIDOW

D

PLAYER E   PLAYER D   PLAYER C

Above: After the deal, no one has exchanged his hand for the widow, so it is turned face up for all players to see before play begins.

CONCLUSION

Depending on the scoring method agreed, a game ends when one player has won all or an agreed number of the chips, or has lost the five chips with which he started.

OTHER COLLECTING GAMES

Games such as Go Fish and Authors are closely related. Their simplicity makes them ideally suited to children. In each, the aim is to collect 'books' – that is, sets of four cards of the same rank – by players asking each other for cards they think might be held. Whoever collects the most books wins the game. The American game Authors gets its name from the fact that, in the 19th century, children played it with cards depicting famous authors. The idea has been extended to include inventors, US presidents, and even well-known baseball players. It is played like Go Fish, but without the stock pile.

GO FISH

You will need: 52 cards	
Card ranking: None	
Players: Three to six	
Ideal for: 4+	

OBJECT

To get rid of all of one's cards, by collecting books of four cards of the same rank (i.e. four Tens, Aces or Jacks), or to score more books than any other player.

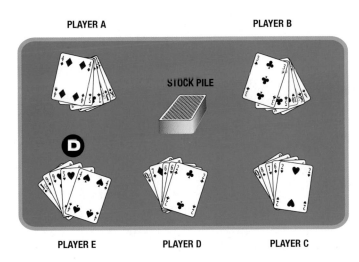

PLAYER A   **PLAYER B**

STOCK PILE

PLAYER E   **PLAYER D**   **PLAYER C**

Above: After the deal, Player A asks Player D for a Seven, as he holds one in his own hand and wishes to collect a 'book'. Player D must surrender his 7♦.

THE DEAL

Although special packs of Go Fish cards are available, a standard card pack may be used as a substitute. Five cards are dealt face down to each player, the remainder being placed face down to form a stock.

PLAY

The player to the dealer's left starts the game by asking another player for a card of the same rank as one that appears in his hand. If the player asked does hold such a card (or cards), he must give it (or them) to the asking player, who then gets another turn. If the responding player does not hold any cards of the requested rank, he responds with 'Go Fish!'

The asking player then draws the top card of the stock. If this card matches his initial request, the asking player shows it and gets another turn. If not, the turn passes to the player who said 'Go Fish!', although the asking player must keep his new card. When a player has a book, this must be shown and put aside.

CONCLUSION

The game ends when a player has no cards left and therefore wins, or the stock runs out, in which case, the player who has collected the most books wins.

AUTHORS

OBJECT

To get rid of all one's cards or score more books than any other player

You will need: 52 cards	
Card ranking: None	
Players: Three to six	
Ideal for: 4+	

THE DEAL

The entire pack is dealt singly as far as it will go. Some players may therefore have more cards than others.

PLAY AND CONCLUSION

Each player in turn asks any other player for all the cards they have of a specific rank, or alternatively for a specific card, such as the 7♣. The player who asks must have at least one card of the solicited rank in his own hand. If the player who is asked holds the card, he surrenders it to the asking player, who then gets another turn. If not, he replies 'None' and takes over the turn. When a player gets all four of a given rank, he lays the cards down in a won trick to show the other players.

The game ends when all cards are formed into books. The player with the most books wins. Alternatively, players score a point per book and play to a target score.

4 | FISHING GAMES

FISHING GAMES PROBABLY ORIGINATED IN CHINA, SPREADING FROM THERE TO JAPAN AND KOREA, WHERE THEY REMAIN POPULAR. THEY ARE ALSO WIDELY PLAYED IN TURKEY, GREECE AND ITALY, ALTHOUGH, FOR SOME REASON, THEY HAVE GENERALLY FAILED TO CATCH ON IN THE REST OF THE WORLD. THE IDEA IS TO MATCH THE CARDS HELD IN THE PLAYERS' HANDS WITH THOSE TURNED FACE UP IN A LAYOUT ON THE TABLE.

There is a straightforward difference between Eastern and Western games of this ilk. In the Eastern games (a classic example being Go Stop, a Korean game that is played with flower cards), there is generally a face-down stock, from which players draw. In Western games, cards are played only from players' hands, although a single card can be used to 'capture' several cards simultaneously if their ranks add up to the rank of the card that was played. If a player cannot match a card or cards, he has to add a card to the layout, or to those cards that are already on the table. This card is now ready for the next player to capture or 'catch' it.

Casino is probably the best known fishing game, and is played particularly in the USA and parts of Scandinavia as well as southern Africa, where specific variations have developed in South Africa, Swaziland and Lesotho. In all these variations, however, captured cards remain in play and so can be recaptured and used in 'builds'. Builds are the most complex features of both Eastern and Western fishing games. They take advantage of the rule that a numbered card can capture its fellows on the table, if they are all of the same rank as the card being played. The intention to play such a card must be announced in advance, with its number specified; after this, the cards can be placed together to form the build. Only by playing a numbered card of the rank that was announced when the build was made can another player capture it.

Above: Flower cards are used in Japan and Korea for games of the fishing group. There are 48 cards in a pack, four for each month of the year.

CASINO

Although Casino is generally thought to have originated in Italy, the first evidence of it being played comes from late 18th-century London and subsequently from Germany.

You will need: 52 cards, but only part of the pack is used in any one deal

Card ranking: None

Players: Best with two to four people, the latter playing in opposing partnerships

Ideal for: 10+

OBJECT

To capture opponents' cards by playing a card matching a layout card's number (pairing) or by playing a card that matches the sum of several such cards (summing).

THE DEAL

Each player is dealt four cards, two at a time, with a further four being dealt face up. The dealer sets aside the remaining cards for use in subsequent deals, but no more cards are dealt to the table.

PLAY

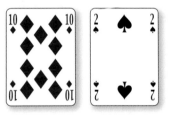

Above: In Casino, the 10♦ is known as the Big Casino and the 2♠ as the Little Casino.

Each player in turn, starting with the one to the dealer's left, plays a card to the table, either capturing one or more table cards or building a combination for capture on a subsequent turn. There are three options during play: to capture, build or trail.

- Capturing – if a player plays a King, Queen or Jack that matches the rank of a card on the table, he can capture that card. If there is more than one matching card on the table – two Queens, say – only one may be captured. A numbered card can capture cards of the same rank and any sets of cards that add up to the rank of the card played. Capturing all the cards on the table is a sweep, which is worth a point to the player making it.
- Building – there are two kinds of build – single and multiple. If a player adds a Three to a Three on the table and announces, 'building Threes' for instance, this is a single build. A multiple build is when more than one card is added. If a player holds two Sixes and there are two Sixes on the table, he plays a Six to the table, puts all three Sixes together, announces 'building Sixes' and captures the combination with the fourth Six on the next turn. The danger of building combinations of cards to be captured subsequently is that an opponent may capture the combination first.

- Trailing – playing a card without building or capturing, when a player can't match any cards in the layout.

SCORING

Only captured cards score. The most valuable are Spades, Aces, the 10♦ (Big Casino) and the 2♠ (Little Casino). At the end of a hand, whoever has the most Spades wins a point. Aces are worth one point each, while Big Casino is worth two points and Little Casino one point. Capturing more than half the pack is worth three points.

The simplest way of scoring is to treat each deal as a separate game. Alternatively, the first player to score 11 points wins a single game, the total being doubled if it takes two deals and quadrupled if this score is accomplished in only one deal.

A third method is known as 21 Up, which is to agree that the first player to win 21 points wins the game, regardless of how many deals it takes.

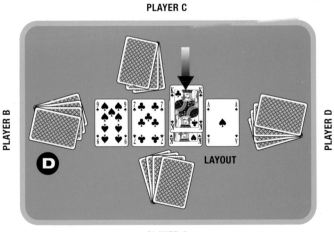

Above: Player C matches the King in the layout, and so captures it.

CONCLUSION

The game ends when all cards have been played with none remaining in stock, and scores are totalled.

ZWICKER

This popular fishing game from northern Germany originated in the area of Schleswig-Holstein, close to the Danish border. The *Zwick* is the name given to a sweep capturing all the cards on the table.

You will need: 52 cards, to which it is customary to add three (or sometimes four) Jokers

Card ranking: None

Players: Two to four – ideally four playing in partnerships of two

Ideal for: 10+

OBJECT

To capture cards from the layout on the table by playing a card of matching value, and whenever possible score bonus points for *Zwicks* – sweeps that clear all the cards on the table.

MATCHING VALUES

Fixed matching values determine which cards can capture which. Cards from Two to Ten rank at face value, but Aces, Jacks, Queens and Kings have two possible matching values of one or 11, two or 12, three or 13 and four or 14, respectively. The player who captures such a card, plays it to capture other cards, or makes it part of a build, decides the value. If a Queen counts as 13, it can be used to capture a Six and a Seven or a Two, Three and Eight and so on. The three Jokers – Small, Middle and Large – are valued at 15, 20 and 25, respectively. Players agree in advance which Joker is which.

THE DEAL

To start the game, four cards are dealt singly to each player, plus two face up on the table.

PLAY

The player to the dealer's left starts by playing one card face up, next to the two face-up cards on the table. When everyone has played, the dealer deals another four cards to each player, none to the table, and so on until a final deal of five cards each exhausts the pack.

If a player plays a card that matches a card on the table, that card may be captured. Two or more such cards can be captured by 'summing', that is, taking cards that have matching values adding up to the matching value of the card being played. To form a build, a player announces its value and then places his card half over the layout card.

Any build counts as though it is a single card – hence, a Five and Seven makes a build of 12, which can be captured by a Jack. No build can be higher than 14. A build's player is obliged to capture the build eventually, unless another player captures or modifies it first.

SCORING

The values used in scoring differ from those used in matching. The small, medium and large Jokers gain five, six and seven points, respectively; the 10♦ is worth three; and the 10♠, 2♠ and each Ace are worth one. These are the only cards that score. A player capturing more than half the cards in the pack scores three points, and each *Zwick* is worth a point. The highest score wins.

Left: Here, a player captures the 6♠ and 7♣, matching their combined total with the Q♠, which has a matching value of three or 13.

CONCLUSION

Once the final deal (of five cards) has been played, the hand is scored.

Left: The 10♦ is worth three points; the 10♠, 2♠ and each Ace are worth one point.

CUARENTA

In Spanish, *cuarenta* means 'forty'. And it is also the number of cards in the deck used in this game and the number of points needed to win it. What distinguishes Cuarenta from most other fishing games is that matching a card also allows cards in sequence with it to be captured.

You will need: 40 cards (Eights, Nines and Tens having been removed from a standard pack)

Card ranking: None

Players: Two or four in two partnerships. In the latter case, one partner keeps score while the other stores the won cards

Ideal for: 10+

OBJECT

To capture cards by matching them. Alternatively, in the case of numbered cards, to capture them by addition, or by forming an unbroken ascending sequence.

THE DEAL

To choose the first dealer, the cards are shuffled and then dealt face up singly to each player. The first player to be dealt a Diamond becomes the dealer. Five cards are then dealt to each player, the remaining cards being stacked face down on the table.

PLAY

After a deal, a player can make an announcement. If a player is dealt four cards of the same rank (Four of a Kind), the cards are shown (announced) and that partnership wins the game immediately. If a player is dealt three cards of the same rank (Three of a Kind), he calls '*Ronda*' and the declaring partnership scores four points. Although the *Ronda's* rank need not be declared, if one of its cards can be captured by *Caida* – by matching it immediately after it has been played – the opposing partnership scores 10 points if they can remember the event and the rank of the cards at the end of the hand, which is when the bonus can be claimed.

At the start of play, or in the case of *Limpia*, a clean sweep of the table, there is obviously nothing to be captured. The card that was played, either at the start of play or to make *Limpia*, simply remains on the table, as do subsequent cards if no capture is made. *Limpia* is worth two points to the side that is making it.

Left: Three of a Kind is called *Ronda* and scores four points for the declaring partnership.

SCORING

The practice is to use the Eights, Nines and Tens to mark scores – these cards otherwise have no function in the game. When face up, each card represents two points, a face-down card, a *Perro* (dog), represents 10 points. Scoring combinations and card plays are:

- *Ronda* (Three of a Kind) – four points to the declaring partnership.
- *Caida* (capturing a card from *Ronda* by matching it immediately after it has been played) – 10 points to the opposing partnership, claimed at the game's end.
- *Limpia* (a clean sweep of the table) – 2 points to the side making it.
- A team with 20 captured cards scores six points (if there is a tie, only the non-dealing partnership scores).
- If more than 20 cards have been captured, each extra card is worth another point, the total being rounded up to the nearest even number.
- If neither partnership captures 20 cards, the one with the greater number scores two points.
- A partnership with 30 or more points cannot score for *Rondas* or *Caidas*, while one that has 38 points cannot collect for *Limpia*. Game is 40 points.

Above: In Cuarenta, the partnership with Four of a Kind wins immediately.

CONCLUSION

At the end of a hand, each partnership counts its collected cards and scores are calculated.

SCOPA

Originating in Italy around the 18th century, *scopa* means 'sweep' or 'broom'. It is still one of the country's major national card games.

OBJECT

To capture as many cards as possible, particularly Diamonds and high-numbered cards.

THE DEAL

Starting with the player to the dealer's right, each player is dealt three cards face down, after which the dealer deals four cards face up to the table. If the table cards include two or more Kings, it is usual to deal again.

PLAY

Each player in turn, starting with the player to the right of the dealer, attempts to capture one or more of the cards on the table. Only one capture may be made in a turn. If there is no capture, the card played becomes part of the layout and may be captured. There is no obligation to play a card that makes a capture. It is sometimes better to simply add a card to the table. If, however, the card that is played does make a capture, the captured cards must be taken. When everyone has played out their three cards, they are dealt three more, and so on, throughout the game, as long as any cards remain.

CAPTURING

The simplest form of capturing is 'pairing', where one card matches another – a Five and another Five, for example. The second form is 'summing', where the value of the card played is the same as the sum of two or more cards on the table. A Seven can capture a Five and a Two. If there is a card on the table which has a value that is the same as the card being played, only that card may be captured. Only one combination may be captured at a time.

A *Scopa* (sweep) is made when only one card is on the table and a player captures it by pairing, or when all the cards are captured by summing. Although a *Scopa* is worth only one point, its additional value is that it leaves the table empty of cards, so forcing the next player to trail (place a card down without matching it). This leaves the way open for another sweep. The 7♦ is the most important card to capture, as it is worth one point and features in the other three points that may be won.

You will need: Italian 40-card pack or standard pack with Eights, Nines and Tens removed

Card ranking: None

Players: Scopa started off as a game for two, but can be played by three or four

Ideal for: 10+

SCORING

Players sort through their won cards and count their scores. A *Scopa* is worth one point. Single points are also awarded for capturing the most cards, for winning the most Diamonds, capturing the 7♦ – the *Sette Bello* (Best Seven) – and for building the best *Primiera*, in which each player extracts from his won cards the highest-valued card he has taken in each suit.

In order to establish which player's *Primiera* is best, the cards are given special values for this particular purpose. Sevens, the most valuable cards, are worth 21 points, Sixes 18, Aces 16, Fives 15, Fours 14, Threes 13 and Twos 12. The three court cards count for 10 points each. The winner of the point is usually the player with the most Sevens in his *Primiera*.

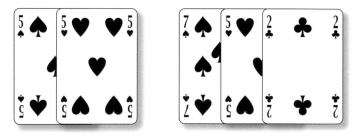

Above: Cards can be captured by pairing, or by summing, the Seven corresponding to the combined value of the Five and Two.

CONCLUSION

Play continues until no cards remain in hand and the stock is exhausted. Any cards left on the table go to whichever player made the last capture, although this does not count as a *Scopa*. The winner is the first player to score 11 points, or the highest score if more than one player has exceeded that figure. If the scores are tied, the points made on the last deal are counted in strict order, starting with cards and then continuing with points for Diamonds, *Sette Bello*, *Primiera* and *Scopa*.

SCOPONE

This partnership version of Scopa also emerged some time in the 18th century, and is recommended to players seeking something different to the standard trick-and-trump games.

You will need: Italian 40-card pack or standard pack with Eights, Nines and Tens removed	
Card ranking: None	
Players: Four, in partnerships of two	
Ideal for: 10+	

OBJECT

To capture as many cards as possible, particularly Diamonds and high-numbered cards, within partnerships.

THE DEAL

Four players sit crosswise, in partnerships. Nine cards are dealt to each player in three batches of three, four cards for the table being dealt two and two after the first and second batches. In Scopone Scientifico (Scientific Scopone), each player is dealt 10 cards, in which case the game has to start with a discard.

PLAY

The rules governing playing, capturing and scoring are broadly the same as in Scopa (see opposite). Partners are not allowed to let each other know which cards they hold in hand, although they can try to signal their intentions by making specific discards in certain situations, such as deciding it is best to avoid capturing a card in favour of trailing one to the table. Captured cards and the cards that captured them are conventionally kept face down in a single pile in front of one of each partnership's players. The first to play – the player to the dealer's right – has to choose the value of the card he plays carefully so as to reduce the chances of it being captured.

SCORING

If a partnership captures more than 20 cards, it wins a point. If the scores are tied, the point is not given. A partnership with five or more Diamonds also gains a point, with an extra point being awarded for the capture of the 7♦. Each *Scopa*, or sweep of the table, is worth a point, while the partnership with the best *Primiera* (the highest-valued card taken in each suit from the won cards) also scores one for it. The first partnership to score 11 or more points wins the game.

In Scientific Scopone, the target is 21 points. Other differences are that a partnership with the A♦, 2♦ and 3♦ scores *Napoli*, a bonus equal to the value of the highest Diamond in the sequence. A partnership that captures all 10 Diamonds – termed *Cappotto* – wins the game outright.

CONCLUSION

The game is over when a partnership scores the specified number of points, according to the version being played.

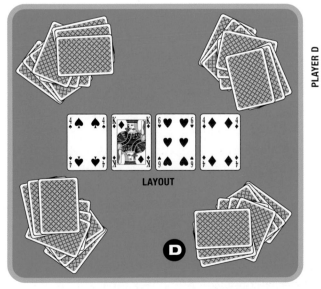

PLAYER C

LAYOUT

PLAYER D

PLAYER B

PLAYER A

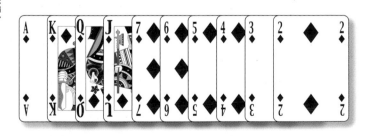

Above: In Scientific Scopone, a partnership that succeeds in capturing all 10 diamonds scores *Cappotto* and wins the game outright.

Left: In Scopone, three cards are dealt to each player, two to the table, or layout, then three more to each player, two more to the table and finally three more to each player. The player to the dealer's right is first to play.

CICERA

Scopa and Scopone have spawned varying rules and options over the years. Cicera, from the Italian province of Brescia, is the most notable variation to have developed.

You will need: Brescian 52-card pack
Card ranking: None
Players: Four, in partnerships of two
Ideal for: 10+

OBJECT

To capture as many cards as possible, aiming to be the first partnership to score 51 points.

THE DEAL

Each player receives 12 cards, with four being dealt face up to the table.

PLAY

Each player in turn plays a card to the table and makes a capture or leaves it on the table. Capturing is by pairing or summing numbered cards (one to 10 at face value), or pairing court cards.

Making a capture is optional, while if the card played matches a single card and the sum value of several cards, its player can choose which to capture. Once all the cards have been played, the last to capture takes any remaining cards.

SCORING

Points can be scored by *Scúa* (a sweep that captures all the cards on the table in one turn), *Picada* (matching the card previously trailed or left on the table), by an opponent, *Simili* (capturing a card of the same suit) and *Quadriglia* (capturing a set of three or more cards). The side with the majority of cards scores two points, as does the one with the most Spades.

Napula, which is *Napoli* in Scientific Scopone, scores three points, while capturing the 2♣, the 10♦ and the J♥ is worth a point for each capture. Game is 51 points.

CONCLUSION

The game ends when a partnership scores 51 points.

CIRULLA

The preferred version of Scopone in the Ligurian region around Genoa, Cirulla has several quirks.

You will need: Italian 40-card pack or standard pack with Eights, Nines and Tens removed
Card ranking: None
Players: Four, in partnerships of two
Ideal for: 10+

OBJECT

To capture as many cards as possible, aiming to be the first partnership to reach the agreed target score.

THE DEAL

Each player is dealt three cards, and four are dealt face up to the table.

PLAY

Each player in turn plays a card to the table and makes a capture or leaves it to trail. As well as pairing and summing, cards can be captured by 'fifteening' (capturing with a card that makes 15 when added to the cards it captures).

SCORING

If the four cards dealt by the dealer total 15, the dealer scores for a sweep. If they total 30, the score is two sweeps. If the cards dealt to a player total less than 10, the player knocks by showing them. This counts as three sweeps or 10 points if they are three cards of the same rank. The 7♥ may be used as a wild card, which can replace any card.

Players score a point for each sweep, for most cards and most Diamonds. Capturing the 7♦ is worth a point, as is *Primiera* (won by the player with the highest-valued cards taken in each suit in his won cards). *Scala Grande*, the King♦, Queen♦ and J♦, scores five, and *Scala Piccola*, the A♦, 2♦ and 3♦, scores three. If the 4♦ is also held, the score is the value of the highest Diamond held in unbroken sequence. Target scores can be 26, 51 or 101.

CONCLUSION

Capturing all the Diamonds wins the game. The game ends when the agreed target score is reached.

BASRA

This fishing game is widely played in coffee houses throughout the Middle East, sometimes under different names. There are Lebanese, Iraqi and Egyptian versions – the last is described here.

You will need:	52 cards
Card ranking:	None
Players:	Two; or four, in partnerships of two
Ideal for:	10+

OBJECT

To capture as many table cards as possible, aiming to be the first partnership to reach the agreed target score.

THE DEAL

Each player is dealt four cards. Four more cards are dealt face up to the table. These are the 'floor' cards and must not include any Jacks or the 7♦. If they do, the offending cards are buried in the pack and replacements are dealt.

PLAY

The player to the dealer's right plays first. Each player in turn plays a card face up to the table, the aim being to capture some of the cards that have already been exposed. When the players have all played their first four cards, they are dealt another batch of four each (no more are dealt to the table) and so on until the entire pack has been dealt. The hand is then scored.

CAPTURING

A player can capture by pairing (matching one card with another) or summing (capturing two or more number cards which have a combined value that is the same as that of the card being played).

As Kings and Queens have no numerical value, only pairing may capture them. If a card is able to capture, a capture must be made, but there is no obligation to play such a card.

Capturing all the cards from the floor at once is a *Basra* and scores a bonus 10 points. Playing a Jack also sweeps the table, but does not count as a *Basra* and therefore no bonus is awarded.

If a 7♦ is played, however, it does count as a *Basra*, provided that all the cards on the table are number cards with a combined value of 10 or less. If it is more than 10, or if there are court cards on the table, the Seven still captures all the cards, but there is no bonus.

SCORING AND CONCLUSION

After the last card has been played, any remaining cards are taken by the last player to have made a capture. Each team counts its cards. A team with 27 or more scores 30 points. If there is a tie, the points are carried forward.

Each Jack and Ace is worth one point, the 2♣ scores two and the 10♦ scores three. Generally, whichever side scores 101 or more points first wins the game. If the score is tied, the convention is to play the final game up to a total of 150 points. The game ends when a partnership wins a rubber (five games), or at an agreed time or points total.

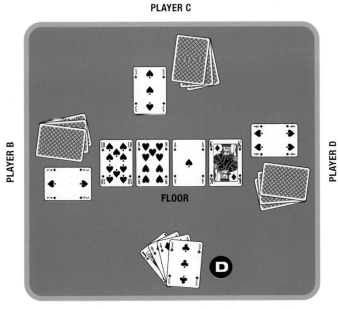

PLAYER C

PLAYER B

PLAYER D

FLOOR

PLAYER A

Above: Player A, the last to lay to this trick, could play the 4♦, matching Player D's 4♣, or the 3♣, matching Player C's 3♠. Playing his Jack, he would be able to sweep all the cards from the floor, but this would not count as a *Basra*.

Right: Neither the 7♦ nor the J♣ may be among the face-up cards on the table at the start of the game, but they are both useful during play for capturing cards.

CHINESE TEN

No coverage of fishing games would be complete without an Eastern example such as Chinese Ten. The way a card is flipped from the face-down deck after each play is typical.

You will need: 52 cards; no Jokers	
Card ranking: None	
Players: Two to four	
Ideal for: 10+	

OBJECT

To achieve as high a score as possible, before all the cards on the stock pile are exhausted.

THE DEAL

Depending on the number of players involved, the number of cards dealt varies. If there are two players, they receive 12 cards each; three players receive eight cards each and four players receive six cards. The next four cards are dealt face up to the table and the rest are stacked face down to form the stock.

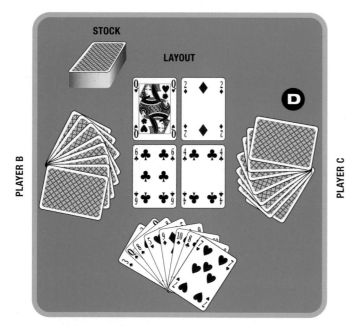

STOCK

LAYOUT

D

PLAYER B

PLAYER C

PLAYER A

Above: In this three-player hand of Chinese Ten, Player A (Player C having dealt) can play either the 8♠ or 8♣ to make a value of 10 when added to the 2♦. Alternatively, the Q♠ could be paired with the Q♥.

PLAY

Each player in turn, starting with the player to the left of the dealer, plays a card to the table. To capture a number card, the card played must make up a value of 10 when added to it. For example, an Ace captures a Nine, or a Nine an Ace, and so on. Only pairing can capture Tens and court cards – Ten takes Ten, Jack takes Jack, and so on. At the end of a turn, having either captured a card or trailed, which is to simply place a card on the table, a player then turns the top card of the stock face up. If this captures a card, both cards are taken. If not, it is left on the table for subsequent capture. You can only play one card per turn. Upon making a capture, you place both cards face down in front of you.

SCORING

Players sift all the red cards from their winnings. Low red number cards score at face value, red Nines to Kings score 10 points each, and red Aces score 20. Black cards do not count when two people play. When three or four play, the A♠ counts 30 extra points and the A♣ scores 40 points.

The score is the difference between points taken and the predetermined 'tie' score, which is set at 105 for two players, 80 for three, and 70 for four. For example, in a game between two players, if the points taken are 119 and 90, the former scores +14 and the latter scores -15.

CONCLUSION

The last card from the pack should always capture the last card from the layout. All 52 cards should end up distributed among the players' winning piles.

Left: The red cards in Chinese Ten score at face value, except for Aces (which score 20) and Nines to Kings (which score 10).

LAUGH AND LIE DOWN

A real oddity, Laugh and Lie Down is the oldest fishing game on record and the only one from English sources. Its name is attributed to players laughing at those who must 'lie down'.

You will need:	52 cards; gambling chips/counters
Card ranking:	None
Players:	Five
Ideal for:	10+

OBJECT

To make Pairs and Mournivals (Four of a Kind) by matching the cards lying face up on the table.

THE DEAL

Before the deal, each player stakes two chips to the pot and the dealer three chips. Each player receives eight cards, and the remaining 12 are dealt face up to the table. The dealer takes any Mournivals among them.

PLAY

Any player with a Mournival in hand 'wins' those cards and places them face down on the table in front of him. If a player holds a Prial (Three of a Kind), he can do the same with two of the cards. The third is retained in hand.

In turn, each player plays a card to the table to make a capture by pairing. This can also be done by spotting other players' oversights. If, for instance, a player captures only one table card when there are three available, the first opposing player to spot this can take the other pair. If a player cannot make a capture he places his hand face up and drops out of play. This is called 'lying down'.

SCORING

The last player left in a hand wins five chips. A player capturing fewer than eight cards pays a chip for every two cards of the shortfall to the pot. However, a player with more than eight cards receives a chip for every two cards he has gone over.

Left: A Mournival (Four of a Kind). After the deal, any Mournivals found among the table cards are promptly won by the dealer.

CONCLUSION

Play continues until only one player has any cards left in hand, after which chips are settled.

Below: Player D holds a Prial (Three of a Kind) and can place it on the table at the start of play, placing two of the cards face down, and keeping the third card in hand. Player C makes a Mournival of Queens from the two in his hand and two on the table.

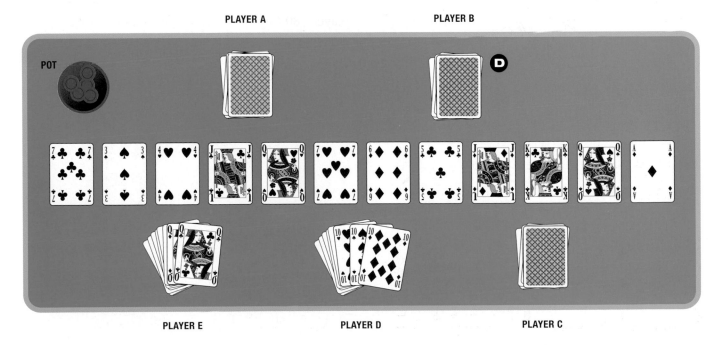

5 | ADDING GAMES

THESE ARE ARITHMETICAL GAMES, WHERE THE AIM IS TO REACH OR AVOID SPECIFIC POINT TOTALS. IN A VARIATION OF NINETY-NINE, PLAYERS ARE PENALIZED IF THEY PLAY A CARD THAT CROSSES ONE OF THE THREE 'BORDERS' – 33, 66 AND 99. HISTORICALLY, SUCH GAMES HAVE BEEN MORE POPULAR IN EASTERN EUROPE THAN THE WEST, THE EXCEPTION BEING CRIBBAGE, BRITAIN'S NATIONAL CARD GAME.

Cribbage's history dates back to at least 1630, if not before. Although its invention was, for a long time, credited to Sir John Suckling (1609–42), a notable poet, playwright and wit of the day, there is now little doubt that it actually derived from a game called Noddy, which was popular in the previous century.

The game's fame quickly grew and spread as it was taken up by monarchs and their courtiers. Catherine the Great of Russia, for one, was an enthusiastic Cribbage player, until Whist and then Bridge supplanted it in aristocratic favour. However, it still flourishes in British pubs and clubs; it is estimated that, in Britain alone, there are two million active tournament players. There are two main versions – Six-card Cribbage, which is the standard, and Five-card Cribbage, a game that is older and now far less widely played. They count as adding games because, in their initial stages, the value of the cards played by both players cannot exceed 31.

Ninety-eight, Ninety-nine and One Hundred are similar adding games. In them, the values of the cards are added together as they are played, the aim being to avoid exceeding the target score.

Noddy and Costly Colours are both curiosities. The former appears to date from Tudor times, although the first descriptions date from more than a century later. And, even in its heyday, Costly Colours seems to have been played only in a fairly limited area in Britain.

Above: Russian Empress Catherine II, also known as Catherine the Great, who ruled from 1762–96, was an enthusiastic cribbage player.

NODDY

The undisputed ancestor of Cribbage, dating back to the 16th century, Noddy is so called after the title given to the Jack of the suit turned up at the start of play. 'Noddy' means a fool or simpleton – one who tends to 'nod' off at any opportunity.

OBJECT

To score 31 points over as many deals as necessary, scores being pegged on a board, just as in Cribbage.

THE DEAL

Players cut for the deal, the one with the lower card dealing first. It then alternates. Each player receives three cards singly, the rest of the pack being placed face down on the table, and the top card is turned up. If it is a Jack, the non-dealer pegs two points for 'Jack Noddy'.

PLAY AND SCORING

After the deal, each player in turn announces and scores for (but does not reveal) any combinations that can be made up from his three cards and the turn-up. A Pair pegs two points, a Pair Royal (three of the same rank) pegs six and a Double Pair Royal (four of the same rank) scores 12. Two or more cards totalling 15 points pegs a point for each constituent card, as does three or more cards totalling 25 and four cards totalling 31, known as Hitter.

PLAYER B

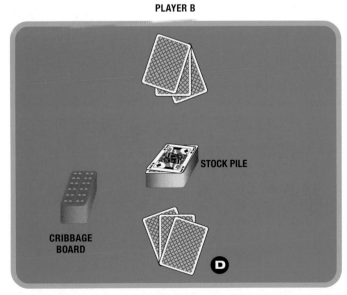

PLAYER A

Above: Non-dealer, Player B, scores two points for the Jack Noddy having been turned up.

You will need: 52 cards; no Jokers; Cribbage board

Card ranking: Standard, Ace low

Players: Two

Ideal for: 7+

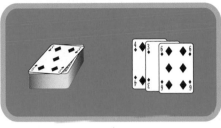

Left: Here, the turn up card of the 5♦ means that player A not only completes a run of four (worth three points) but also pegs four more points for a four-card flush.

PLAYER A

Three consecutive cards, such as Two, Three and Four, peg two, and four consecutive cards peg three. Flushes – three or more cards of the same suit – peg a point per card. If the Jack was not turned after the deal, then Jack Noddy is the Jack of the same suit as the turn-up card, and its holder (if any) pegs a point for it.

Any card can be counted more than once, provided that it forms part of a separate combination on each occasion. If either player reaches 31 points from the combination of cards that he holds in his hand, then the game ends and there is no play-off.

If neither player attains 31 points, then the game proceeds to a play-off. The non-dealer plays a card to the table, announcing its face value. The dealer plays in turn, announcing the combined value of the two cards. In the play-off, Aces count for one point, numbered cards count at face value, and court cards score 10 points each. The process continues until 31 points have been pegged, or until neither player can continue without busting (exceeding 31 points).

If one player can continue to play while the other cannot, he plays on alone. If 31 is exceeded, the player who last kept it under 31 pegs one point.

CONCLUSION

Once 31 has been scored – which can happen before a card has been played, when the players announce their combinations – the game is over. Any cards left in hand do not score.

Six-Card Cribbage

Whether Six-Card or Five-Card, Cribbage stands out as a unique game. A special Cribbage board is required to play, which uses pegs to record scores. Much of its terminology is also quaint, examples including phrases such as 'one for his nob' and words like 'skunked', used to describe a losing player.

You will need:	52 cards; Cribbage board
Card ranking:	Standard, Ace low
Players:	Two
Ideal for:	7+

Object

To score as many points as possible in each hand, being the first after several hands to peg out (complete two circuits of the Cribbage board).

The Deal

Both players cut for the deal, the one with the lower card dealing first – Aces are low. Both players, starting with the non-dealer, receive six cards singly. The remaining cards are stacked face down on the table as the stock.

Above: If any Jack is turned up after cutting the pack, the dealer immediately pegs two points 'for his heels'. If a player has a Jack in their hand that is the same suit as the turned-up card, they peg one point 'for his nob' when hands are shown.

The Discard

After the deal, both players discard two cards face down to form the crib of four cards, aiming to keep a hand that forms scoring combinations. The four crib cards are put aside until the end of the hand, when the cards in it count for the dealer.

The non-dealer cuts the stock. The dealer takes the top card of the bottom half and puts it face up on the top of the pack. This card is the start card. If it is a Jack, the dealer can peg two points, known as 'two for his heels'.

Play

Starting with the non-dealer, each player takes it in turn to play a single card, placing the cards in separate face-up piles. They score a running total, the value of each card being added as it is played.

Each time 31 is reached (players must not go above this), the score goes back to zero and another round starts. When a player plays a card that brings the total exactly to that figure, he claims 'thirty-one for two' and pegs two points. If a player cannot play without going over the total, he says 'go' and allows the opposing player to continue. If neither can play, the last player to do so pegs 'one for the go and one for last'. Play goes on until all the cards in hand have been played.

PLAYER B

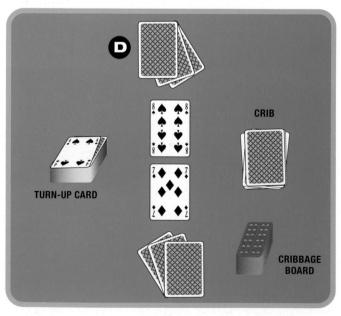

PLAYER A

Above: This hand pegs 22 points. There are seven combinations of Fifteen (three times with each Jack, and all the Fives added together), making 14 points, together with a Pair and a Pair Royal (giving two and six points respectively).

Left: Player B lays an Eight after the initial lead of a Seven. The two cards add up to 15, so Player B calls 'fifteen for two' and is able to peg two points.

PLAYER B

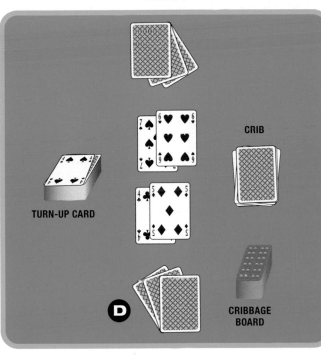

TURN-UP CARD

CRIB

D

CRIBBAGE
BOARD

PLAYER A

PAIRS AND RUNS

If a player makes any of the following scores in addition to the ones that have already been described, he can peg them immediately. If a card is played that brings the total to 15, its player claims 'fifteen for two' and pegs two points. If a card of the same rank as the previous one is played, the score is 'two for the pair'. If a third card of the same rank is played immediately after this, it is a Pair Royal and its player pegs six points. A 'Double Pair Royal' is awarded if a fourth card of the same rank is played, its player pegging 12 points.

A run is a sequence of three of more cards of consecutive ranks, irrespective of their suits. A player completing a run pegs for the number of cards in it. If, for instance, a Four, Two, Six, Five and Three are played, the player of the Three scores five for a five-card run.

Above: This hand pegs 18 points. There are four combinations of 15, making eight points, together with a run of four yielding four points and a flush, giving five points. Finally, there's another point 'for his nob'.

Left: Player B played first here, laying the 7♠. Player A responded with the 4♣. Player B then played the 6♥, allowing Player A to lay the 5♦ and peg four points for a run of Four, Five, Six, Seven.

THE SHOW (SCORING)

Once all the cards have been played, each player picks up the cards they have played and scores them, the start card being counted as part of the hand for both players.

The combinations and scores (shown in brackets) are:

- Fifteen (2): two or more cards totalling 15, counting Ace as one, numbered cards at face value, court cards as 10.
- Pair (2): two cards of the same rank.
- Prial or Pair Royal (6): three of the same rank.
- Double Pair Royal (12): four of the same rank.
- Run (1 per card): three or more cards in ranking order.
- Flush (4 or 5): four or more cards of the same suit.

The same card can be counted as part of different combinations. If a hand contains a Jack of the same suit as the start card, one 'for his nob' is pegged. Finally, the dealer turns over the crib – the four cards the players discarded between them after the deal – and scores it as a five-card hand, exactly as above.

CONCLUSION

The first player to peg out – to exceed 121 points – wins the game. This can happen at any time during play as long as the opposing player's pegs are still on the board. It is usual to play the best of three. If the losing player's score is less than 91, he is 'lurched' or 'skunked' and forfeits double. If it is under 60, it is a 'double lurch' or 'skunk' and he forfeits triple.

Above: A special Cribbage board and pegs are needed to record the scores in Cribbage. There are two pegs – the forward one showing a player's current score and the rear peg the previous score.

FIVE-CARD CRIBBAGE

Five-card Cribbage was, for a long time, the standard version of the game and it still features in club, tournament and championship matches, probably because it is partner-friendly.

OBJECT

To be the first to peg 61 points. A player pegging fewer than 45 points is 'in the lurch'.

You will need: 52 cards; Cribbage board	
Card ranking: Standard, Ace low	
Players: Two	
Ideal for: 7+	

THE DEAL, PLAY AND SCORING

Four players play as partners, each being dealt five cards and discarding one to the crib. The player to the dealer's left leads first and makes the first show.

At the start of play, the non-dealing partnership pegs 'three for last' as compensation for not having the benefit of the crib.

Hands are played only once until 31 has been reached. Any cards left over remain unplayed.

Four cards of the same suit (a Flush) in hand pegs four – five with the turn-up card. A Flush in the crib (the four cards discarded by players after the deal) only pegs five if it matches the turn-up card's suit.

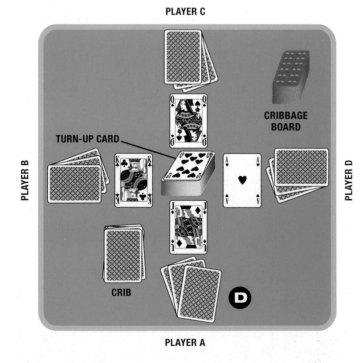

Above: In Five-Card cribbage, if 31 points have been reached, no more cards are laid. Hand points are now calculated.

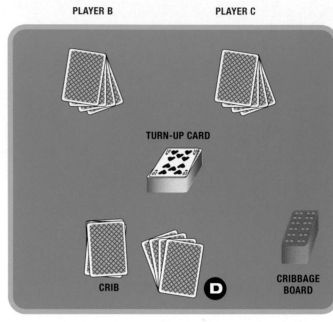

Above: In Three-Handed Cribbage, each player receives five cards and one is dealt for the crib. Players must each make one discard, bringing each hand, including the crib, up to four cards.

VARIANTS

In the cut-throat version of Three-Handed Cribbage, each player receives five cards, followed by one to the crib. Players then discard a card each to the crib, after which the player to the dealer's left cuts the pack to reveal the turn-up and plays first. He also shows and counts first, the last player to do so being the dealer. Each player scores for himself.

In the solo version, the dealer's two opponents play as a partnership, each receiving five cards. The dealer takes six cards. Both partners then pass a card to the dealer, who discards four cards to the crib. Play is the same as in the cut-throat game, the one main difference being that each partner scores the amount made by them both. The same applies in Four-Handed Cribbage.

Losing Cribbage is a two-handed six-card game. It is played as the standard version, but the main difference between the two is that every score a player makes is credited to their opponent. The first to score – or rather not to score – 121 points, wins.

In Auction Cribbage, each player states how many points he will subtract from his score in return for the crib, before the starter is turned. The highest bidder deducts that amount and play proceeds as usual.

COSTLY COLOURS

Noted for its complex scoring, Costly Colours is probably a cousin of Cribbage, but relatively little is known about it. Charles Cotton was the first to describe it in his *Complete Gamester*, of 1674. It seems to have survived up to Victorian times, but is no more than a historical curiosity.

You will need:	52 cards; Cribbage board
Card ranking:	Standard, Ace low or high
Players:	Two
Ideal for:	10+

OBJECT

To be the first player over a series of games to reach 121 points, by making sequences, combinations and other scoring card plays.

THE DEAL

Both players receive three cards singly, the next card – the deck card – being turned up. Both players use it to help to make sequences and combinations. If it is a Jack or a Two, the dealer pegs four points 'for his heels'.

PLAY

Before play, each player can 'mog', that is, pass a card from his hand face down to the other player. If a player refuses, the other pegs a point for the refusal. If a player mogs (gives away) a Jack or Two, he may first peg two points for it, or four if it is the same suit as the deck card.

The non-dealer plays a card face up to the table, followed by the dealer, who then announces the combined value of the two cards. Play continues until 31 points are scored, or either player cannot play without exceeding that total. This is termed 'busting'. The first player unable to play without doing this has to say 'go', after which the opposing player may add as many cards as possible before he, too, busts. He scores an extra point for the go, plus a point per card if he manages to score 31 exactly. Both players then reveal their cards and peg the value of their scoring combinations, the non-dealer pegging first. The convention is for declarations to be made in the following order – points, Jacks and Twos, Pairs and Prials, Colours and Flushes (see Scoring).

If either player is left holding cards in hand, the cards played so far are turned down and removed from play. The next in turn to play then starts a new series.

SCORING AND CONCLUSION

Fifteen, 25 and 31, scored in play or in hand, are one point each, a Pair pegs two points, a Prial (Three of a Kind) pegs nine and a Double Prial (Four of a Kind) pegs 18. A Jack or Two of the turned-up suit pegs four; any other Jack or Two pegs two.

Sequences count only in play (one point per card) while Colours (reds or blacks) count only in hand. Three in Colour pegs two; Three in Suit pegs three; Four in Colour, Two in Suit pegs four; Four in Colour, Three in Suit pegs five; Four in Suit – Costly Colours – pegs six. The first to reach 121 points wins.

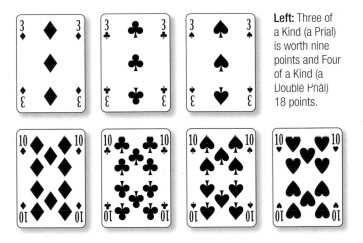

Left: Three of a Kind (a Prial) is worth nine points and Four of a Kind (a Double Prial) 18 points.

Below: With all four cards the same colour, and three of the same suit, this combination would score five points (Four in Colour, Three in Suit). Had the 9♦ been a 9♥, this would have made Costly Colours (four cards of the same suit), scoring six points.

Left: If a Jack or Two is turned up as the deck card, the dealer pegs four points.

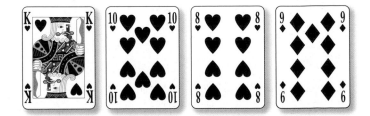

NINETY-EIGHT

This is the first of a set of games known as Adders, in which the card values are added together during play. The aim is to score a set number of points, or to avoid specific totals.

You will need: 52 cards
Card ranking: See 'Play and Scoring', below
Players: Two or more
Ideal for: 7+

OBJECT

To avoid taking the value of the pile above 98.

THE DEAL

Each player receives four cards dealt singly, the remainder being placed face down on the table to form a stock. Players play their cards face up to the table to create a pile alongside the stock.

PLAY AND SCORING

The player to the dealer's left plays first, with play continuing clockwise around the table. At the moment a card is played to the pile, its player calls out the pile's cumulative value and then draws the top card of the stock to replace the card that was played.

Certain cards change the value of the pile. Playing a Ten reduces its value by 10 points. If a Jack or Queen is played, the value stays the same, whereas playing a King immediately sets the value at 98. All other cards simply add their face value.

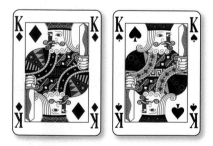

Left: In Ninety-eight, if a King is played, the value of the pile is immediately set at 98.

CONCLUSION

The first player to take the pile above 98 is the loser and, according to convention, has to buy the other players a round of drinks or do a forfeit.

NINETY-NINE

Said to be a Gypsy game, Ninety-Nine is played along similar conventions to its sister game Ninety-Eight, with some notable exceptions.

You will need: 52 cards; gambling chips/counters
Card ranking: See 'Play and Scoring', below
Players: Up to four
Ideal for: 7+

OBJECT

To avoid taking the value of the pile above 99.

THE DEAL

Up to four players start with five chips each and receive three cards from a standard 52-card pack. The remaining cards are placed face down on the table to form a stock.

PLAY AND SCORING

The player to the dealer's left plays first and play proceeds clockwise. Each player plays a card face up to a pile on the table, calling out the cumulative value of the pile as they do so. They each then draw the top card of the stock as a replacement.

For each card played, the pile's value goes up by the value of the card, Jacks and Queens counting for 10 points each. An Ace increases the pile's value by one or 11 points, as decided by its player. If a Four is played, the pile value stays the same, but the direction of play reverses. A Nine is worth nothing.

After a Four or Nine, the player calls out the existing value of the pile, saying 'pass to you' or 'back to you', respectively. Playing a Ten increases or decreases the pile's value by 10 points at its player's discretion. Playing a King immediately makes the pile's value 99. Each player loses a point every time they play a card that crosses one of the three 'borders' – 33, 66 and 99.

CONCLUSION

A player unable to play without taking the pile's value above 99 lays down his hand and tosses a chip into the centre of the table. A player with no chips left drops out of the game. The last player left with any chips, wins.

One Hundred

In certain variations of Adders games, there are individual cards that have special effects; in One Hundred, for instance, playing the A♠ doubles the value of the card pile.

You will need: 52 cards; gambling chips/counters

Card ranking: See 'Play and Scoring', below

Players: Three to six

Ideal for: 7+

Object

To get rid of all your cards without taking the value of the pile above 100.

The Deal

Three cards are dealt one at a time to each player. The remainder is placed face down on the table to form a stock.

Play and Scoring

Play starts with the player to the dealer's left and proceeds clockwise around the table. Cards are played singly face up to form a pile, each player calling out its cumulative value as they play, before drawing the top card of the stock to replenish their hands.

A King is worth nothing. The Queens are worth 10 – except for the Q♥, which sets the pile value at zero. Playing a Jack reduces the pile value by 10. Playing a Ten raises the pile value to 100. Most number cards count at face value. Playing a 2♠ doubles the pile value; playing a Four reverses the direction of play. Playing a red Five decreases the pile value by five points. Playing an Ace from a black suit means that its player can set the pile value at any figure between 0 and 100.

If a player makes the pile value equal 100, the only cards the next player can play are black Aces, Fours, red Fives, Tens, Jacks, the Q♥ or Kings.

Conclusion

A player unable to play without taking the pile's value above 100 lays down his hand and tosses a chip into the centre of the table. Players drop out if they lose all their chips; the last with any chips is the winner.

Jubilee

In this Czech game, played with a 61-card pack, the cards in the black suits score positive points, while those in red suits count as minus points.

You will need: A 61-card pack, containing one full Hearts suit, two Spades suits, two Clubs suits from Ace to Nine (Tens and court cards discarded) and four Jokers

Card ranking: See above, and under Play, below

Players: Two to seven

Ideal for: 10+

Object

To win the most of the 189 points available.

The Deal

Each player is dealt eight cards, the remainder of the pack being placed face down on the table to form a stock.

Play

Starting with the player to the dealer's left, each player in turn plays a card to a common waste pile. The first to play must play a black card and announce its value. As the players play more cards, they must announce the total value of all the cards that have been played so far in the game. Once they have played a card, they draw replacement cards from the stock, and the procedure continues until the stock is exhausted. No one may bring the total score down to zero. Any player unable to make a legal play must show his hand and pass.

Scoring

Any player who is able to make the running total an exact multiple of 25, by addition or subtraction, scores 10 for a 'Jubilee'. If the total is also a multiple of 100, this score is doubled to 20. But, if a player causes the total to 'jump' a Jubilee rather than hitting it exactly, whether by addition or subtraction, he is penalized five points. It is against the rules of the game to bring the total to below zero.

Conclusion

The game ends when the last card has been played. The final total should be 189 points.

6 | SHEDDING GAMES

THE AIM OF THESE GAMES IS TO GET RID OF CARDS AND TO BE THE FIRST PLAYER TO GO OUT. IN SOME, CARDS MUST BE PLAYED IN ASCENDING SEQUENCE, USUALLY IN SUIT. IN OTHERS, PLAYERS MUST MATCH THE RANK OR SUIT OF THE PREVIOUS CARD PLAYED. ELEUSIS, DEVISED BY GAMES INVENTOR ROBERT ABBOTT IN 1956, IS UNIQUE. PLAYERS SHED CARDS BY MATCHING, BUT THE RULES GOVERNING THIS PROCESS, KNOWN TO ONLY THE DEALER, MUST BE DEDUCED BY OTHER PLAYERS.

Games belonging to the 'Stops' group require that cards be played in ascending order, but also that there is no set order of play. Whoever holds the best card plays it. The 'stops' are the cards that are left undealt and never drawn. This obviously makes it harder to play, since it stops the sequence from following its logical course. In such games, all players are trying to get rid of cards from their hands by playing one or more cards to a discard pile, aiming to match or beat the previous card played.

The oldest of such games is Huc, which was around in the 16th century, followed by Comet a century later. The curiously named Pope Joan game was a middle-class Victorian favourite. The most popular modern game is Michigan, as it is called in the USA. It started off life in Britain as Newmarket.

There are many games within the specific group of shedding games known as 'eights games', but their fundamental objective is the same – to match the rank and suit of the previous card played. Some games are more elaborate than others. In Bartok, for example, the rules about which cards count for what vary from hand to hand. In Eleusis, the dealer invents the rules governing play and the other players try to deduce what it is by noting which plays the dealer rules are legal and which are illegal.

Other games in this group such as Zheng Shangyou and President are known as 'climbing games', as each player in turn tries to play a higher-ranked card than preceding players.

Above: American games inventor Robert Abbott devised the game of Eleusis, which he described as a 'game of inductive reasoning', in 1956.

DOMINO

This long-established game goes by various names, including Card Dominoes, Fan Tan, Parliament and Spoof Sevens.

You will need: 52 cards; no Jokers; gambling chips/counters

Card ranking: None

Players: Any number, but ideally six or seven

Ideal for: 7+

OBJECT

To be the first player to get rid of all one's cards by playing them to a layout on the table.

THE DEAL

Dealer cuts the pack, dealing all the cards out singly to the players. Play starts clockwise from the dealer's left.

PLAY

Before play starts, each player pays an agreed number of chips into the pot. The first to play must then play a Seven – the suit does not matter – or pass. In the latter case, the penalty is a chip to the pot and the turn passes to the next player. Assuming a Seven has been played, that player must play the Six of the same suit to the left of the Seven, the Eight of the same suit to the right, or any other Seven above or below it. The next to play must play another Seven, or the next higher or lower card of the suit sequence. The aim is to end up with four rows of cards,

each consisting of 13 cards of the same suit, with the Ace at the far left and the King at the far right. It is best to play Aces or Kings as soon as possible. At each point, if a player cannot go, he must pass and pay a chip.

SCORING

Anyone who fails to play when able to do so, forfeits three chips to the pool. A player who fails to lay a card when he could have played a Seven, forfeits three chips to the pool and five to the holder of the Six and Eight of the suit in question. The first player to get all their cards out scoops the pool. He also collects a chip for each card left in hand from all the other players.

CONCLUSION

The game ends when a player lays the last of his cards.

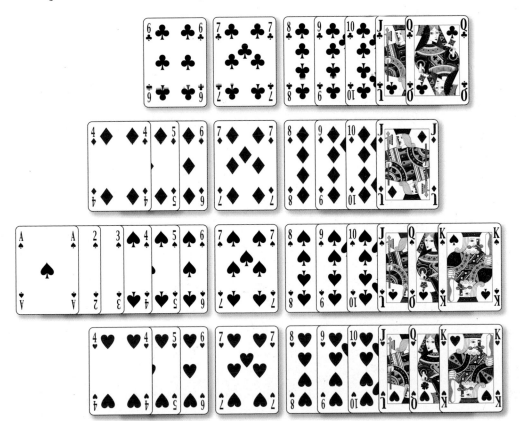

Above: After players have paid an agreed number of chips into the pot, each game has to begin with a Seven being played.

Left: The rows are all well on their way to completion and it's a race now to see who can play their last card first.

MICHIGAN

Also known as Stops, or Boodle, this game is probably descended from the gambling games enjoyed by the 17th-century French nobility, although it is far less serious and the stakes are by no means as high. In Newmarket, the original British version, Aces are low.

OBJECT

To be the first player out, winning stakes by playing specific cards along the way.

BETTING

Before the deal, players stake a certain number of chips on four cards, which are the only ones taken from a second pack, placed face up in the centre of the table to

Above: The four 'pay' cards, or boodle cards, (those that pay out) in Michigan are the A♥, K♣, Q♦ and J♠.

Left: Cardinal Mazarin, pictured here, was an avid card player, and was thought to have used gambling games to his advantage as a 17-century politician in France.

You will need: Two 52-card packs; no Jokers; gambling chips/counters

Card ranking: None

Players: Three to eight

Ideal for: 7+

form a layout. The cards in question, A♥, K♣, Q♦ and J♠, are termed 'boodle' cards or 'pay' cards. The dealer stakes two chips on each card and the other players a single chip on each. (In one variant, each player is allowed to distribute his chips freely among the boodle cards, rather than having to stake a fixed amount on each one).

THE DEAL

Each player deals in turn, the deal passing to the left after a hand. All the cards are dealt one at a time, the last card of each round going to form a spare hand, left face down on the table. There are no fixed numbers of cards required to be dealt – the pack is simply dealt out one card at a time to each player. It does not matter if some players get one more card than others.

The dealer can exercise the option of exchanging the hand he was dealt for the spare one. He cannot look at the spare hand before deciding whether to make the exchange – this must take place sight unseen. If the decision is not to exchange, the dealer can auction the spare hand – again, sight unseen – to the highest bidder. Whichever player buys the hand must pay a fixed stake to the kitty. The dealer, however, can exchange his hand for

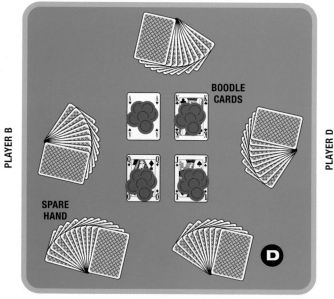

PLAYER C

BOODLE CARDS

PLAYER B

PLAYER D

SPARE HAND

D

PLAYER A

Above: If the dealer decides not to exchange the spare hand for his own, and no one else buys it from him in order to exchange it for his own hand, it is left face down on the table.

the spare one for nothing. If no one wants to bid, the spare hand is left where it is and it takes no further part in the game. Evidently, whoever deals gets a slight advantage, so the usual practice is to end a game only after all players have had the chance to deal the same number of times.

PLAY

Starting with the player to the dealer's left, each player in turn plays a card face up to the table, announcing what the card is as it is played. Cards that have been played are kept in front of the person who played them until the end of the hand.

The suit that is led depends on which version of the game is being played. In some, any suit may be led, but others specify that Clubs or Diamonds must be played first. Whichever version is followed, the lowest card held in that suit must be led. Whoever holds the next highest card of the same suit must then play it, followed by the next highest, and so on. A player holding more than one card in an ascending sequence may play them at the same time. If, for instance, a player holds the Three and Four of Diamonds, he can play both simultaneously.

During the course of play, any player who plays a card that matches one of the boodle cards wins all the chips staked on that card. The total number of chips staked is usually a set number, but how they are distributed varies. Play continues until either the Ace is played, or no one

PLAYER A

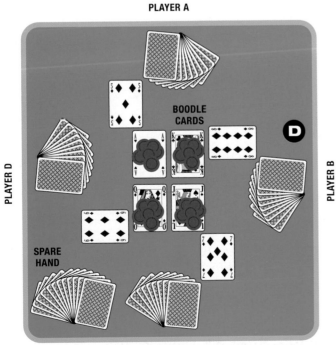

PLAYER C

Above: The 8♦ is the last card laid, so the 9♦ is needed next.

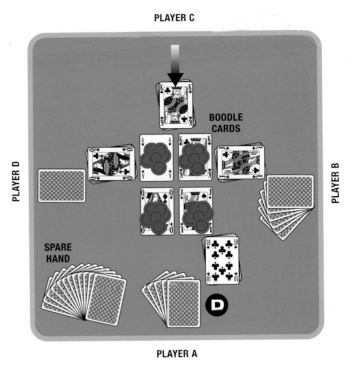

Above: Player C can lay his last card, the K♣, thus receiving gambling chips from other players for each card they hold in their hands – Player C receives two gambling chips if they are boodle cards.

holds the next card in sequence, usually because the card needed has already been played or is in the spare hand. A stop card is one that no one can follow. The last person to play then starts a new round of play. Any suit can be played and the card played must be the lowest one held in that suit, followed by the next one in sequence, and so on.

In one variation of the game, the suit led to restart the game must be different to the previous one. Some versions insist on black after red and red after black. If the player who ended play in the preceding sequence cannot play a card with a different suit, the turn to play passes to the player to his left.

CONCLUSION

There are two possible conclusions. The first is when no one can play another suit, in which case the game ends in a stalemate and there are no forfeits for any cards left in hand. Otherwise, as soon as one player runs out of cards, play finishes. All the other players forfeit a chip for each card remaining in their hand – two chips if any of the remaining cards are unplayed boodle cards. The chips go to the winner. Any chips remaining on the table stay there, the stakes being carried forward to the next hand.

CRAZY EIGHTS

When it appeared in the 1930s, this game was called simply Eights. It developed its new name as it became more elaborate. Alternate names include Crates and Swedish Rummy. In Germany, it is Mau Mau (Mao in the USA), in Switzerland Tschausepp and, in the Netherlands, Pesten.

OBJECT

To discard as quickly as possible by matching the number or suit of the previous player's discard.

THE DEAL

The dealer deals five cards singly to each player (seven if only two are playing), the remainder being placed face down on the table to form a stock. The top card of the stock is turned up and placed beside it to start a discard pile. If it is an Eight, it is buried in the stock and the next card is turned up to take its place.

PLAY

The player to the dealer's left plays first. Each player in turn must discard a card on to the discard pile. To do so, the card has to match the rank or suit of the previous discard. If this is impossible, the player concerned must draw a card from the stock or, if the stock has run out, pass.

You will need: 52 cards; no Jokers
Card ranking: None
Players: Two to five (or more, using two packs combined)
Ideal for: 7+

Eights are wild cards. An Eight can be played on any card, its player then nominating the suit that must be played next. It need not be the same suit as the Eight. Some other cards also have a special significance, depending on what form of the game is being played. Sometimes, for instance, playing a Queen means that the next player has to skip his turn, while playing an Ace reverses the direction of play from clockwise to anti-clockwise, and vice versa.

SCORING

If a player gets rid of all his cards, the others score penalties according to the cards they have left in hand. An Eight scores 50, a court card 10 and number cards count at face value. An Ace scores one. If no one can match the last card played, the player with the lowest combined value of cards in hand wins and the remaining players are penalized the respective difference between the value of the cards they hold and the winner's.

CONCLUSION

Play stops when one player has got rid of all his cards or no one can match the last card played, after which scores are calculated.

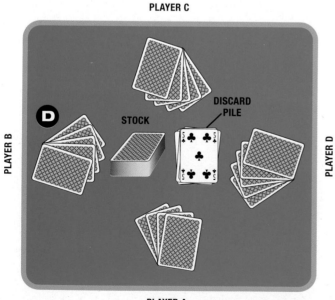

Above: Player B, to play, must lay a card of the same rank (another Five) or suit (another Club) or draw a card from the stock.

Above: If an Eight is turned up, it is buried in the stock and a new card turned up instead.

Left: In Crazy Eights, cards numbered Two to Six and Nine count against players at face value. Eights, however, count as 50, court cards as 10 and Aces as 1.

SWITCH

Also known as Two-Four-Jack or Black Jack, this elaboration of Crazy Eights became so popular in the 1960s and 1970s that it gave rise to a proprietary game called Uno, which is played with special cards of its own.

OBJECT

To be the first player to get rid of all your cards.

THE DEAL

Players receive 12 cards if two or three are playing, but otherwise the deal is 10 cards each. The remainder are stacked face down to form a stock, and the top card is turned face up and placed next to it to start the discard pile. This is the start card for the first sequence of cards.

PLAY

Starting with the player to the dealer's left and continuing clockwise, each player plays a card of the same rank or suit as the previous one face up on top of the discard pile. The alternative is to play an Ace. This is a wild card and its player can specify the suit that must be played next.

If a player cannot play with the cards in hand, he must draw from the stock until he can play. Once the stock is exhausted, all the cards that have been played, with the exception of the last hand, are gathered up, shuffled and laid down as a new stock.

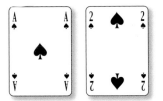

Left: Playing an Ace entitles a player to specify the suit to be played next. Playing a Two forces the next player to play another Two or draw two cards.

Left: A Four must be met with another Four, failing which, four cards are picked up. A Two on a Two or a Four on a Four doubles the penalty cards the next player must pick up, and so on. A Jack switches the direction of play.

TWOS, FOURS AND JACKS

- Playing a Two forces the next player to either play a Two, or draw two cards from the stock and miss a turn. If the player after that also plays a Two, the fourth person must play a Two as well, or draw four cards and miss a turn. The maximum number of cards that a player can be forced to draw is eight.
- Playing a Four is the same, although the number of cards to be drawn goes up to four, eight, 12 or 16.
- Playing a Jack switches the direction of play.

A player with only two cards left must announce 'one left' as he plays the first of them. Otherwise, he misses a turn and has to draw a card from the stock.

SCORING

Aces score 20, Twos, Fours and Jacks 15, Kings and Queens 10. All other number cards count at face value.

CONCLUSION

The first player to get rid of all his cards wins, scoring the value of the cards left in the other players' hands.

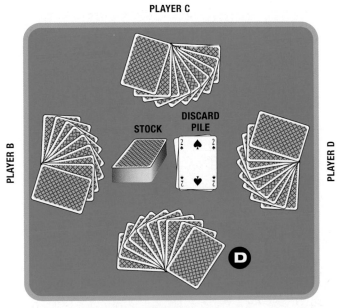

PLAYER C

STOCK

DISCARD PILE

PLAYER B

PLAYER D

PLAYER A

Left: Player D has laid a Two, meaning that Player A, the next to play, must pick up two cards and miss a turn. If Player A holds a Two, he can play it instead of picking up, meaning that Player B, if he does not have a Two, will have to pick up four cards and miss a turn.

You will need: 52 cards; no Jokers

Card ranking: None

Players: Two to seven

Ideal for: 7+

ELEUSIS

This is certainly one of the most mind-bending card games around. Primarily, this is due to the fact that each hand of play is governed by a secret rule, chosen by and known only to, its dealer.

You will need:	Three 52-card packs shuffled together; no Jokers
Card ranking:	None
Players:	Four to eight
Ideal for:	14+

OBJECT

To decipher the dealer's rules and so be the first to get rid of all one's cards.

THE DEAL

The choice of dealer is random, although the convention is that no one deals more than once in the same session of play. Whoever deals receives no cards and does not take part in the game in the conventional way. Each of the other players is dealt 14 cards; then a card is dealt face up on to the table. The remaining cards are stacked face down as the stock.

The dealer's task is to devise a rule governing play that is not too easy or too difficult for the others to deduce and then to enforce it by declaring plays legal or illegal. The rule is never actually revealed during play, although the dealer may choose to give hints as to what it might be. A fairly typical rule would be as follows: if the last card played was from a red suit, the next card to be played must be from a black one, and, if the first card was even, the next card must be odd.

PLAY

The players' aim is to establish a 'mainline sequence' from the starter card across the table to the right, and to get rid of all their cards. A card can be played to the mainline only if it matches the card preceding it. Otherwise, it must be placed in a sideline extending at right angles from the mainline. What is a match varies, depending on the rule each dealer devises. Thus, play is more or less by trial and error until enough evidence has been obtained to suggest what the rule is most likely to be.

As each player plays a card, the dealer calls 'right' or 'wrong'. If the former, the card stays where it was played to the mainline. If the latter, the card is placed in a sideline and the dealer deals the offending player twice the number of cards played – a minimum of two up to a maximum of eight, if the player has tried to play a string of cards.

A player who believes he has discovered the rule, but who has no suitable card to play, can declare 'can't play' and expose the hand, so the dealer can check whether the declaration was right or wrong. If it was right, what happens depends on how many cards are left in hand. If it was wrong, the dealer plays any of the cards that will fit to the mainline and deals the mistaken player five cards. If there are five or more, the dealer places them at the bottom of the stock and deals the player in question four fewer cards than the number they previously held in hand. If there are four or fewer, the game ends.

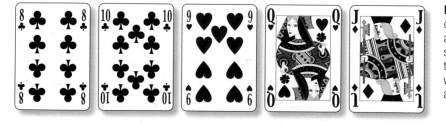

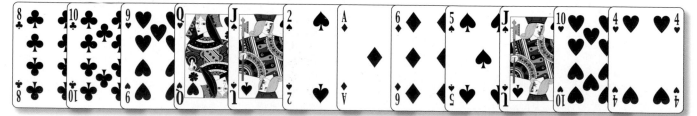

Left and Below: The dealer has devised a rule that cards must go up two in the same suit, then down one to a suit of the opposite colour, then up two in the same suit; then down one to the other red suit; then up four; then down one to the other black suit, and so on. This would make the sequence of cards in the top row acceptable, but that of the row below, unacceptable.

BECOMING 'THE PROPHET'

A player believing he knows the rule may opt to declare himself the prophet in the hopes of bettering his score. There are four conditions:

- The declaration can be made only after successfully adding to the mainline (see 'Play') and before the next in turn starts to play.
- There can be only one prophet at a time.
- No one can be the prophet more than once in a deal.
- At least two other players must still be in play.

The prophet takes over the dealer's functions (telling players if moves are legal or not), and the dealer confirms or negates each decision. If a decision is negated, the prophet is deposed. If there is no prophet, an illegal play means expulsion from the game once 30 cards have been played to the mainline. If there is a prophet, expulsions start once 20 cards have been added to the mainline following the declaration.

SCORING

Every player scores a point for each card left in the hand of the player with the most cards and loses a point for each card in his own hands. A player with no cards in hand wins four points, while the prophet scores a bonus point for every card played to the mainline and two points for each card on any sideline since the declaration.

The dealer scores the same as the highest-scoring player, unless there is still a prophet. If so, the dealer counts the number of cards played since the declaration and doubles the total. If this is less than the highest score, the dealer scores that instead. If the game ends before all players have dealt, those concerned score an extra 10 points each.

CONCLUSION

Play ends and scores are calculated when a player is out of cards, or all, bar the prophet, have been expelled.

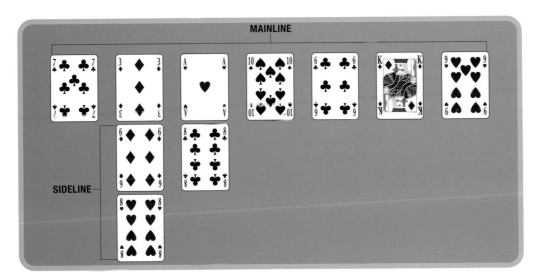
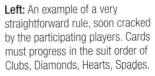

Left: An example of a very straightforward rule, soon cracked by the participating players. Cards must progress in the suit order of Clubs, Diamonds, Hearts, Spades.

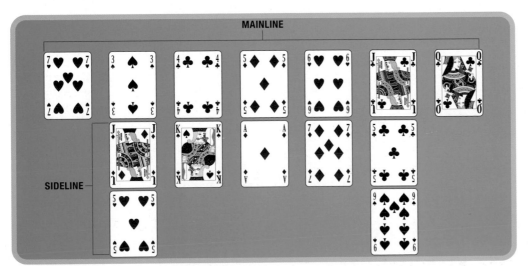

Left: A possible layout on the table during a game of Eleusis. The rule is that, after the first card, a card of the opposite colour must be played next, followed by one of the same colour in sequence. After this, any card of the opposite colour must be played, again followed by a card of the same colour in sequence. Cards breaking this rule are placed in a sideline until the correct card is laid.

POPE JOAN

How this game came to be named after the legendary 13th century female pope is unknown. Traditionally, it was played with a special circular staking board with eight compartments labelled Ace, King, Queen, Jack, Game, Pope (9♦), Matrimony (King and Queen of trumps) and Intrigue (Queen and Jack of trumps). The layout is easy to replicate on paper. Each player starts with a specified number of chips or counters (at least 20).

OBJECT

To be the first player to run out of cards and also to win the most chips.

THE DEAL

The dealer starts by 'dressing the board', which means six chips must be put into the compartment that is labelled Pope, two chips are put into the compartments of Matrimony and Intrigue, and one in each of the other compartments. The cards are then dealt singly to each player, a spare hand also being dealt.

The last card of this hand is turned up for trumps. If it is Pope, Ace, King, Queen or Jack, the dealer wins the contents of the appropriate compartment. The hand plays no further part in the game.

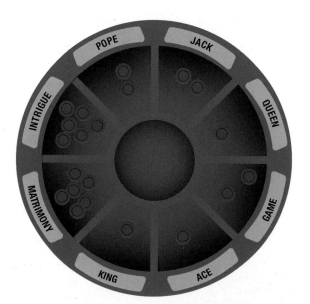

Above: Pope Joan is played on a special staking board with eight different compartments to accommodate the various betting chips, although a makeshift 'board' can easily be reconstructed using paper.

You will need: 51 cards; 8♦ removed; no Jokers gambling chips/counters; paper and pen

Card ranking: See 'Play and Scoring', below

Players: Three to eight

Ideal for: 10+

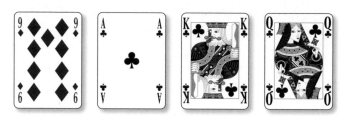

Above: Assuming Clubs are trumps, whoever plays the Ace wins the contents of the Ace compartment of the staking board. The same applies to the Queen and Jack, in their respective compartments. Whoever plays the 9♦ (the Pope) wins the contents of the Pope compartment. Playing the King and Queen of trumps in succession wins the chips in Matrimony, while playing a successive Queen and Jack wins Intrigue.

PLAY AND SCORING

The player to the dealer's left leads with the lowest card of any suit in his hand. Whoever holds the next highest card of the same suit plays it, and so on, until the sequence cannot be continued. An Ace, for instance, is a natural stop card since it is the highest card in the game. Or, the card required may be in the spare hand, or may have been played already. The cards are played face up to the table, where they stay until the end of the game. The last to play starts a new sequence, again with the lowest card held of a suit of his choice.

Whoever plays the Ace, King, Queen or Jack of trumps, or Pope, immediately wins the contents of the relevant compartment. If the Jack and Queen of trumps are played in succession, their player wins Intrigue. Playing the Queen and King of trumps wins Matrimony, while playing all three wins both compartments.

CONCLUSION

The first person to play the last card from his hand wins the game. The winner scoops the contents of the Game compartment and receives a chip for each card still held in hand from the other players, although a player holding an unplayed Pope (9♦) does not have to pay this. Any unclaimed stakes are carried forward to the next deal.

PRESIDENT

Possibly originating in China, President has several names and many variations. The aim is to be the first player to get rid of all one's cards, so becoming the President. The last player left in is the Donkey. The game's peculiarities include rules governing not only where players should sit, but also what they sit on. In most versions of the game, suits are irrelevant.

You will need: 52 cards, in some versions two Jokers are added as wild cards

Card ranking: Two, highest, then Ace down to Three. If the Jokers are added, they outrank all other cards

Players: Four to seven

Ideal for: 14+

OBJECT

To get rid of all one's cards before anyone else.

THE DEAL

All the cards are dealt singly and the game proceeds clockwise around the table.

PLAY

The player to the dealer's left leads, or, alternatively, the player holding the 3♣. This person leads either a single card or a set of cards of equal rank (for example, three Fives). The others can either pass or play the same number of cards as the preceding player – and all of the same rank, which must be be higher than the ones previously played (for example, three Sixes).

The round continues until, after a play, the other players all pass. The last to play may not play again, but must turn, face down, all the cards that have been played, and then lead to the next round. If he has no more cards left, the lead moves round to the next player who has not run out of cards. Play stops when all bar one of the players have run out of cards.

The first player to run out of cards becomes the President, the next player the Vice-President, and so on. The player who is left with a card or cards still in hand is the Donkey. At this point, the President shifts to the most comfortable seat, and the Vice-President to the next most comfortable one. Other players sit according to their winning or losing status, while the Donkey sits to the President's right (on the least comfortable chair) and the Vice-President to the left.

The Donkey now becomes dealer, dealing the first card to the President. Once the deal has been completed, the Donkey and the President exchange a card, the Donkey giving the President the highest card in his hand and getting back an unwanted one. The President leads to the next round.

In other versions of the game, the names given to players vary. At one time in Europe, King, Nobleman, Poorman and Beggar were popular, as were Boss, Foreman, Worker and Bum. In other versions, players are meant to wear appropriate items of headgear.

SCORING AND CONCLUSION

Two points are scored for becoming the President, one for becoming Vice-President; other players score nothing. The first person to score 11 points is the overall winner.

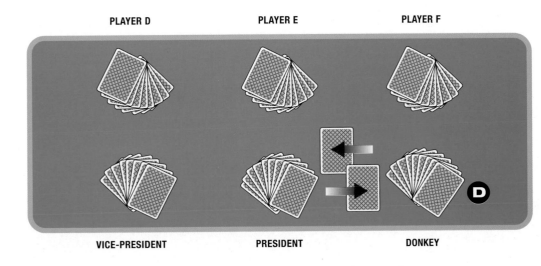

PLAYER D PLAYER E PLAYER F

VICE-PRESIDENT PRESIDENT DONKEY

Above: In this scenario, the 7♦ has been laid, so the next player must lay an Eight or higher.

Left: After a deal, the Donkey gives his highest card to the President, in exchange for an unwanted one.

ZHENG SHANGYOU

In Chinese, this name roughly means 'Struggling Upstream', but in Britain it has been christened Pits, since the losing players become 'pit dwellers'. It is related to several other Eastern games, such as Big Two, also from China, the Japanese game of Dai Hin Min, and Tien Len from Vietnam.

OBJECT

To be the first or second player to get rid of all one's cards. Players drop out as they lose their cards until only the losing player remains with cards in hand.

THE DEAL

The first player to deal is chosen at random, the next to deal being the loser of the previous hand. The dealer shuffles the cards, places them face down on the table and draws the top card. This is followed by the player to the right. The process continues anti-clockwise around the table until the pack is exhausted.

PLAY

The dealer leads the first of a number of rounds of play. He may lead using any of the following patterns:

- A single card.
- A set of two or more cards of the same rank.
- A single sequence of three or more cards of consecutive rank.
- A multiple sequence (this consists of equal numbers of cards of each of three or more consecutive ranks – for example, 55, 66, 77 or JJJ, QQQ, KKK).

Although suits are generally irrelevant, any single suited sequence is better than any mixed suited one of the same length. If two sequences are mixed, the higher ranking one is the better.

Above: A multiple sequence – three paired cards of consecutive rank. This combination would beat any pair, set or single sequence.

You will need: 52 cards and two distinguishable Jokers

Card ranking: When laying single cards or a set, the red Joker is highest, followed by the black, the Twos, then Ace down to Three. For single and multiple sequences, Ace is highest, Three lowest. For Twos and Jokers, see below under 'Wild Cards'

Players: Four or more play as individuals. There is also a partnership version

Ideal for: 14+

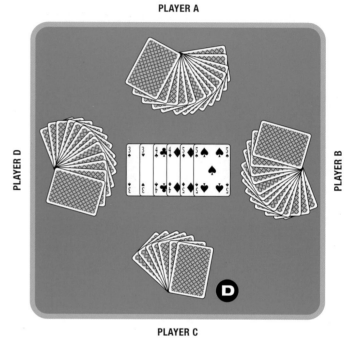

PLAYER A

PLAYER D

PLAYER B

PLAYER C

Above: The dealer has laid a multiple sequence – three paired cards of consecutive rank – thus getting rid of six cards.

Each player now has to decide whether to pass or to play. There is no penalty for passing even if a play could be made – a player can re-enter the game when his turn to play comes round again. The next player must play the same number of cards as there were in the original lead. The cards must also form the same pattern and have to outrank the cards that were in the preceding play. For example, a pair can be followed only by a higher pair, a single sequence by a single sequence of the same length, but with a higher-ranking top card, and so on.

Tactically, the highest priority is to get rid of the low cards as quickly as possible. It is probably best to avoid leading high cards unless, by doing so, a player can see a sure, safe way of getting rid of all his cards. Often, players holding long sequences find it better to split them up and play them as two or more sequences.

Play goes on until all, bar one, of the players opts to pass in turn. At this point, the last to play turns down all the played cards, which are gathered up and set aside. He then starts the game again by leading with a new playable combination. If that player has no cards left, then the lead passes to the right.

WILD CARDS

Subject to certain restrictions, Jokers and Twos can be played as wild cards to stand for any lower cards. A set containing wild cards loses to an equally ranked natural or pure set. Twos cannot be played in single sequences at all. Jokers can stand in for any card from Three to Ace, but a single sequence reliant on a Joker or Jokers can be beaten by a natural or pure sequence. This also applies to multiple sequences. Although Twos are valid wild cards, they cannot stand for all the cards of a particular rank. At least one must be a natural card or a Joker. For example, 55, 62, 77 is legal, but 55, 22, 77 is not.

SCORING AND CONCLUSION

The first player to run out of cards wins that particular hand and scores two points, while the second player to run out of cards, the runner-up, scores one point.

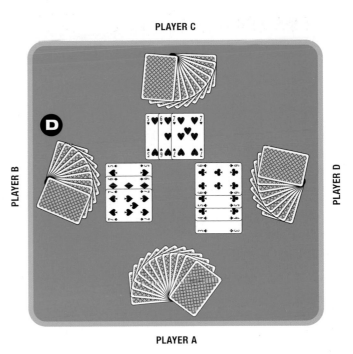

Above: Player B has a mixed sequence of three cards, but Player C beats this with a three-card sequence in the same suit. Player D, however, tops this in turn with a four-card sequence, putting the onus on Player A to lay a higher combination or pass.

No other player can score, although play continues until only one player is left with cards in hand. The last two players become what are known as 'the pit dwellers'. Immediately after the new deal, they must toss their highest-ranking card face up onto the table. If they hold cards of equal rank, they can decide which one of them they prefer to discard. The previous hand's winner is first to pick whichever card he prefers, leaving the second one for the runner-up. Both players then discard one unwanted card each. The second-to-bottom player picks up one of the cards first, leaving the other one for the bottom-placed loser. Play then continues.

The first player to score a total of 11 points wins a rubber. This is card parlance for the match. Typically, it consists of three games and is therefore won by the first player or partnership to win two games.

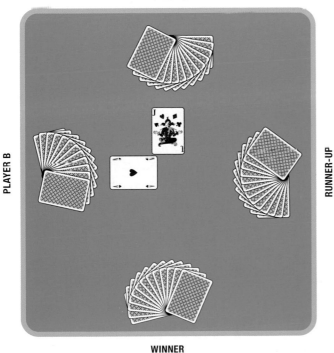

Above: The players who came last and second to last in the previous deal must toss their highest-ranking card face up on to the table. The winner of the previous hand can choose which to pick up, leaving the other card for the runner-up. Both winners discard, and the roles are now reversed, with the second-to-bottom player choosing a card first, followed by the losing player.

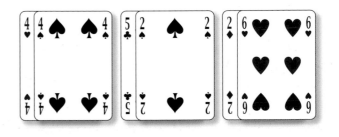

Above: A Two may represent any natural card to accompany an existing card (here Twos represent Five and Six). A Joker may represent any desired card.

Tieng Len

During the Vietnam War, the Vietnamese national card game reached the USA, where, in a slightly adapted version, it became known as Viet Cong or VC. It is a climbing game, in which Twos rank as the highest card. The highest-ranked suit is Hearts, followed by Diamonds, Clubs and Spades. Rank, however, takes precedence over suit, for example, the 8♠ would beat the 7♥.

Object

To get rid of your cards as quickly as possible by beating combinations of cards played by other players. The aim is to avoid being the last player with cards remaining in hand.

The Deal

The first dealer is chosen at random, after which the loser of each deal deals the next game. Cards are dealt one by one, the number depending on the number of players. When there are four, each receives 13 cards; two receive 26; and three receive 17 (the remaining card is left out of play). If more than four play, two packs are used, and the dealer must take care to ensure that an equal number of cards are dealt, and that any left over are discarded.

Play

Initially, the player holding the 3♠ plays first – if no one holds this card, it is the player holding the lowest-ranked card. The 3♠ must be played either on its own or as part of a combination. There are six valid 'combinations' that may be played:

- A single card: the lowest card is the 3♠, while the highest is the 2♥.
- A pair (two cards of the same rank).
- A triplet (three cards of the same rank).
- A quartet (four cards of the same rank).
- A sequence (three or more cards of consecutive rank).
- A double sequence (three or more pairs in which the cards rank consecutively, for example, 33, 44, 55). A sequence cannot 'turn the corner' between Two and Three because Twos are high and Threes low.

In two combinations of the same type, the highest-ranked card in them determines which of the two is the better. Each player now has to play to beat the previously

You will need: 52 cards (two packs if more than four players)

Card ranking: Two (highest), then Ace down to Three

Players: Best for four, although it can be between two and eight

Ideal for: 14+

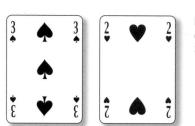

Left: The lowest single card that can be played in Tieng Len is the 3♠. The 2♥ is the highest.

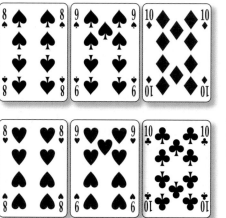

Left: The top three-card sequence would beat that on the bottom, since, when adjudicating between matching sequences, it is the highest-ranking, or top, card that is compared, and Diamonds rank higher in Tieng Len than Clubs.

played card or combination. If a single card is led, only single cards can be played; if a pair, only pairs; and so on. Playing a triplet, therefore, will not beat a pair. Nor will playing a five-card sequence beat a four-card one. A pair consisting of the 7♥ and 7♠ beats one consisting of the 7♣ and 7♦, because Hearts are ranked higher as a suit than are Diamonds. Similarly, 8♠, 9♠, 10♦ beats 8♥, 9♥, 10♣, because it is the Tens that are being compared and Diamonds rank higher than Clubs.

Generally, a combination can only be beaten by one of the same type. However, there are four specific exceptions involving beating Twos, as indicated on the opposite page.

Passing is allowed, even if a player, in fact, could play a card or cards. However, if a player passes, he must continue to pass throughout that round of play. Play continues around the table, omitting players who have passed until another player makes a play that no one else can beat. When this happens, all played cards are set aside and the player whose play was unbeaten starts play again.

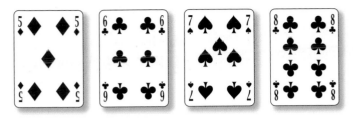

Above: If a four-card sequence is laid, then the next player must also lay a four-card sequence to beat it, topped either by the 8 (Hearts being the highest-ranked suit) or by a Nine.

Above: A four-card sequence, topped by a Two, is the highest-ranking denomination in Tieng Len.

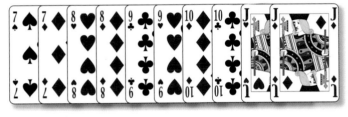

Above: To beat a triplet of Twos requires a double sequence of five, such as the above, a very rare combination.

Beating Twos

There are four exceptions to the rule concerning the play of similar combinations. These all involve beating the play of one or more Twos, the highest-ranked card, as follows:

- A single Two is beaten by a quartet.
- A single Two is beaten by a double sequence of three (for example: 55, 66, 77).
- A pair of Twos is beaten by a double sequence of four (for example: 33, 44, 55, 66).
- A triplet of Twos are beaten by a double sequence of five (for example: 33, 44, 55, 66, 77, 88).

Conclusion

As players run out of cards, they drop out of play. When it comes to their turn to lead, this passes to the next player to the left around the table still with cards in hand. Play ends when only one player has any cards remaining. He is the loser and has to pay a previously agreed stake to each of the other players.

Variants

Variants of Tieng Len are played in the USA under the name of Viet Cong. The rules vary slightly, as follows:

- A player with four Twos automatically wins the game.
- The player who holds the 3♠ initially must play a combination including that card.
- Twos can be included only in double sequences.
- The highest permissible card in a single sequence is an Ace. Single sequences are called straights and run from Three up to Ace.

There are also special combinations, termed slams, which can beat Twos. The rules for these are:

- A double sequence or a quartet beat one Two.
- A double sequence of five or two consecutive quartets beat a pair of Twos.
- A double sequence of seven or three consecutive quartets beat three Twos.

Another variant involves trading cards before the first lead is played. Any player can exchange any number of cards with another by mutual agreement. If there is no such agreement, the trade does not take place; if it does, a quartet of Twos does not automatically win the game.

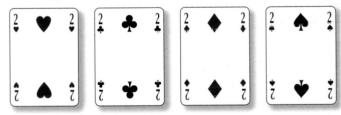

Above: A player with a quartet of Twos in Viet Cong wins the game

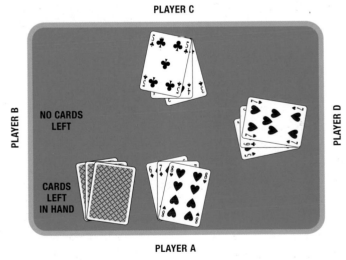

Above: Player B has got rid of his cards so sits out the rest of the hand. Player C lays down a sequence of three, which is topped by Player D and topped in turn by Player A. Players C and D now have no cards left, so Player A is the loser and has to pay an agreed stake to each of the other players.

7 | BEATING GAMES

As a rule, games of this genre are more complex than those discussed so far in this book. In them, players generally take it in turns to be attackers and defenders. Failure to beat an attack means picking up the attacking cards, sometimes others as well, and adding them to your hand. While striving to get rid of one's cards, the primary object is usually to avoid being the last player in, rather than the first one out.

Perhaps the most celebrated example of a game of this kind is Durak, Russia's national card game since Tsarist times. It can be either a multiple or a continuous attack game, in which players take it in turn to attack and defend in what is called a bout. *Durak* means 'fool' and the title is awarded to the player left with cards in hand after all the other players have got rid of their cards.

Shed's origins are uncertain, and it has infinite variations and alternate names. It appears to be closely related to the Finnish game Paskahousu, but unlike the latter, has travelled and is now a favourite in most parts of the Western card-playing world. In all variants, the loser becomes the Shed. He has to perform any menial tasks the other players assign him until someone else succeeds to the role. Elsewhere in Europe, the beating games Rolling Stone and Sift Smoke are both popular.

Mustamaija is another classic beating Finnish game where there is no winner, only a loser. This is the player left holding the Queen when all the other players have run out of cards. A player with the Queen also has to be careful not to play this card too early, or he may be forced to pick it up again. Its holder must therefore carefully judge the best time to play it, which is usually when he thinks that the game is about to end.

Above: An 18th-century Russian woodcut print of two card players. Russia's national card game, Durak, is the most elaborate of the beating games group.

ROLLING STONE

The proverb says that 'a rolling stone gathers no moss', but the opposite can occur here. Players accumulate more cards as the game is played.

OBJECT

To be the first player to run out of cards.

You will need: 52 cards	
Card ranking: Standard	
Players: The game is best for three to six	
Ideal for: 7+	

THE DEAL

Each player receives eight cards. All remaining cards are left unused.

PLAY

The player to the dealer's left leads. Players must follow suit, for example, with Clubs; the first player who is unable to do so takes the played cards and leads to the next round. If everyone follows suit, the highest card wins. The winner discards the trick and leads to the next one.

SCORING AND CONCLUSION

The first player to run out of cards is the winner. He scores the value of all the cards held by other players. Number cards and Aces count at face value and the court cards count as 10 each. When playing with young children, you may prefer to start a new game after each hand.

PLAYER C

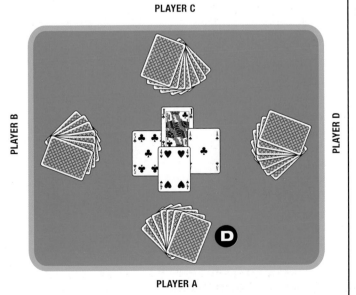

Above: Unable to follow suit after the preceding players have laid Clubs, Player A must pick up the played cards and lead to the next round.

SIFT SMOKE

Also known as Linger Longer and Lift Smoke, this game can be accurately classed as the negative version of Rolling Stone.

OBJECT

To be the last player in, not first one out.

You will need: 52 cards	
Card ranking: Standard	
Players: Three to six	
Ideal for: 7+	

THE DEAL

Players are dealt 10 cards if three are playing, seven if four, six if five, and five if six. The last card establishes trumps.

PLAYER C

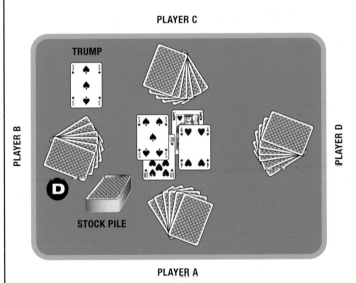

Above: Unable to follow suit, Player B can play a trump and win the trick. The cards in the trick are laid down on the table and will only be used again if new stock is needed. He picks up a card from the stock pile and adds this to his hand, which means he will have a card more than the other players.

PLAY AND SCORING

The rules of play are the same as those of Rolling Stone, except that, if trumps are played, the highest trump wins, not the highest card of the same suit. The trick's winner draws a card from the stock. As players run out of cards, they drop out. The winner scores a point for each card in hand.

CONCLUSION

The last player with cards in hand wins. If the stock runs out before this, previous rounds are shuffled to form a new stock. If all players play their last card to the same round, the round's winner wins the game.

DURAK

There are many versions of this celebrated Russian game, which has no winner – only a loser, or a losing side if the game is played with partnerships. One of the most popular versions of this game is Podkidnoy Durak, a game involving a rule which allows other players to join in an attack after it has started by 'throwing in' more cards of matching ranks to those that have been played.

OBJECT

To be the first player out of cards once the stock is exhausted, but, most importantly, to avoid becoming the *Durak*, or 'fool' with the remaining cards.

THE DEAL

Each of the players is dealt six cards one at a time, the next card being turned face up to determine trumps. The remaining cards are placed face down crosswise over the turn-up, so that its rank and value remain clearly visible. These cards form the stock.

PLAY

Initially, the player with the lowest trump (the Six of trumps or, failing a Six, the Seven, and so on) starts play. This consists of a series of bouts, in which there is an attacker, who, in this version, may be aided by the others, and a defender, who plays alone.

Below: This player has been tricked by the *Durak* (fool) into cutting the pack, so must take on the *Durak*'s role, which involves dealing and cutting cards.

You will need: 52-card pack with Twos to Fives removed

Card ranking: Ace highest, down to Six, lowest

Players: Two to six; or four playing in partnerships of two

Ideal for: 10+

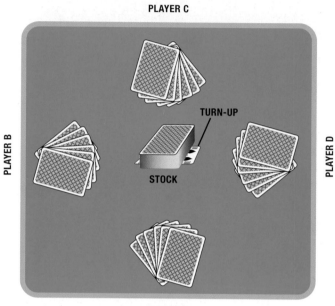

Above: Each player is dealt six cards face down, with the next card turned face up to determine trumps. The remaining cards are placed in a pile face down crosswise over the turn-up card and serve as the stock.

ATTACKERS AND DEFENDERS

The first player is always the attacker, while the player to the attacker's left is always the defender. Although other players can join in an attack, they may do so only with the main attacker's permission, who must indicate whether to go ahead and play, or wait. Before deciding whether to continue with an attack, alone or with others, an attacker also has the right to ask questions regarding another player's proposed attacking cards.

The attacker starts by playing any card face up in front of the defender. To beat off the attack, the defender must play a higher card of the same suit, a trump, or a higher trump if a trump is led. If the defender cannot do this, he must take all the played cards into his hand.

MULTIPLE ATTACKS

If this attack is beaten, more attacks can still be launched, subject to the following stipulations: each subsequent attack card played must be of the *same* rank (it doesn't need to be higher) as a card that has already been played by either the attacker or the defender. The maximum number of attack cards that can be played in any one bout is six. If a defender holds less than six cards before a bout starts, the maximum number of attack cards is the same as the number of cards in the defender's hand.

If a defender cannot beat an attack, he picks up the attack card, together with all the other cards played in the bout until then. All the players entitled to take part in the attack also give the defender the cards they could have played had the attack continued.

Each attack card is placed separately face up in front of the defender, who places each card played in reply on top of it, taking care to position it so that the values of both sets of cards can be seen. A successful defender becomes the new attacker. If the defence is unsuccessful, the role passes to the player to the defender's left, the next player in rotation becoming the next defender.

DRAWING FROM STOCK

After each bout, any player left with fewer than six cards in his hand must replenish it by drawing cards from the stock. Each player in turn, starting with the attacker, takes a card from the stock until either he has six cards or the stock is exhausted with the taking of the trump turn-up. The defender draws last and does not draw if he holds six or more cards. After the stock runs out, play continues without drawing.

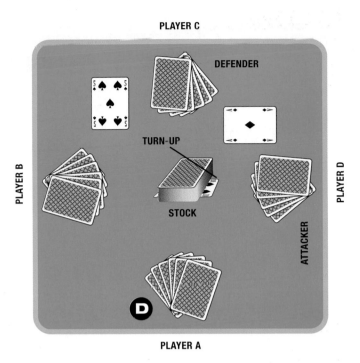

Above: The only defence against Player D's attack (A♦) is to play a trump.

If a player draws the Six of trumps, this card can be exchanged for the turned-up trump, even if another player has already drawn the turn-up, provided that play in the next bout has not yet begun.

ENDING

In the individual version, as each player runs out of cards, he drops out of the game. If the defender's last card beats the attacker's last card, the result is a draw.

In a partnership, if one partner drops out, the other takes over the turn. They decide between themselves which of them will deal the next hand and become the *Durak*, or 'fool'. The other partner will then be the defender. In this scenario, it is often advantageous for the weaker player to deal first, so that the stronger one defends. He may also be able to take advantage of card etiquette.

According to the rules, only the dealer can handle the cards, which is deemed a menial task. If another player can be tricked into touching them – by cutting them, say, after the initial shuffle – that player must take over the dealer's, or *Durak's*, role.

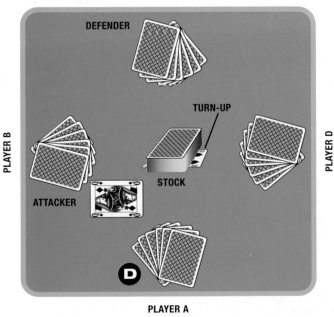

Above: A single attacker, Player B, has led the Q♦. The defender, Player C, must play a K♦ or A♦ or a trump, in this case, a Spade, to beat the attack.

CONCLUSION

Play continues until the last player remains with cards. This player still holding cards is the loser, also known as the *Durak*, or 'fool'.

SVOI KOZYRI

This Russian single-attack beating game seems to have been around since the beginning of the 19th century. Its name means 'one's own trumps', which gives an immediate clue to its chief peculiarity. Before the game, each player chooses a different trump suit, cards of which can trump any other cards of any other suit.

OBJECT

Using trumps to avoid being the last to hold any cards.

THE DEAL

Before the cards are dealt, the players select their trump suits. Each player receives nine cards, dealt singly.

PLAY

Before play starts, the players check their hands to see if they are holding any Sixes of suits other than their personal trump suit. If they are, they give them to the player whose trump suit they belong to, which means that all the players hold at least one trump.

The player to the dealer's left leads any card face up to the table to start a play pile. The other players try to beat the top card of the pile by playing a higher card of the same suit or a personal trump, followed by a second card of their own choosing. It is not necessary to follow suit.

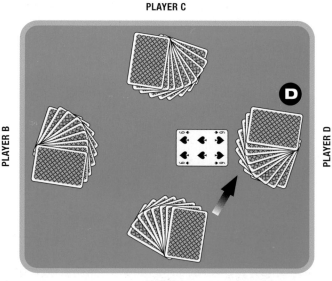

Above: At the start of play, each player who holds a Six that is not of his chosen trump suit must hand it over to whomever has chosen that suit.

You will need: 52-card pack with Twos to Fives removed

Card ranking: Ace highest, down to Six, lowest

Players: Best for four

Ideal for: 14+

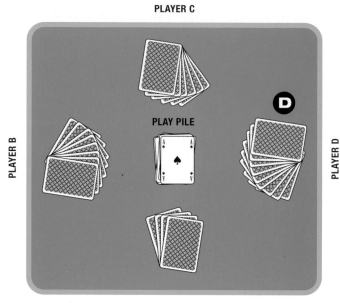

Above: The play pile is topped by an Ace, led by Player A. If this suit happens to be Player B's personal trumps, he must pick up the entire play pile. Players here hold different-length hands, having had to pick up penalty cards during play.

If a player cannot beat the top card, or elects not to do so, he has to pick up from the pile. If the top card is not one of that player's trumps, the pick-up is three cards, or the whole pile if there are fewer than three cards in it. If it is that player's trump other than the Ace, the pick-up is five cards. If it is the Ace of that player's trump, he must pick up the entire pile.

Before deciding whether to play, the player concerned is allowed to look at the cards that would have to be picked up, including the card that the next to play would have to beat. If the previous player takes the whole pile, the next to play starts a new pile. As players run out of cards, they drop out of the game.

CONCLUSION

The last player left holding any cards is the loser. If that player, however, has only one card left and can beat the last top card with it, the game is a draw.

DUDAK

This Czech favourite (translated 'bagpipe') can trace its origins back to Durak and Svoi Kozyri, since it incorporates elements from both games. It is fairly straightforward to play, which is presumably why many children in its Bohemian homeland are said to be addicted to it.

OBJECT

The aim is to play out all of one's cards. The last player left holding a card or cards in hand is the loser.

THE DEAL

Each player is dealt eight cards singly from a 32-card pack.

PLAY

The player to the dealer's left leads, playing any card face up to start a play pile. Subsequently, each player in turn may, if possible, play two cards to the play pile. Before doing so, a player may opt to declare a suit to be personal trumps for the rest of the game. Each player will normally choose a different suit, but it is possible for two or more players to choose the same trump. However, having nominated a trump suit, a player may not change his suit for the rest of the game.

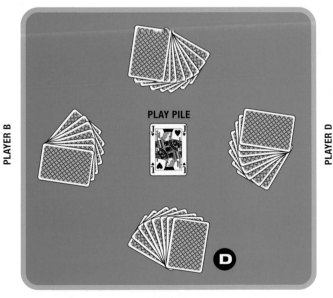

PLAYER C

PLAY PILE

PLAYER B

PLAYER D

PLAYER A

Above: Player B here, the first to play following Player A's deal, has led the J♥. Player C now must lay Q♥, K♥ or A♥, or a trump if trumps have been declared, after which he can lay a second card of his choice.

You will need: 52-card deck with Twos to Sixes removed

Card ranking: Ace highest, to Seven, lowest

Players: Best for four

Ideal for: 14+

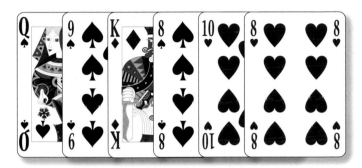

Above: With Clubs as trumps and the Q♥ topping the pick-up pile, a player holding this hand would be unable to beat or trump it. He would therefore have to pick up all the cards from the pick-up pile.

The first card to be played must be a higher card of the same suit as the top card of the pile, or a trump, if trumps have been declared. The choice of the second card is up to each player. If a player cannot beat the top card, or elects not to, he must pick it up and continue to pick up cards until one that he can beat or one which he is willing to beat, is uncovered. If the whole pile is taken, that player's turn ends and the next player starts a new pile.

If a personal trump suit has been declared, the procedure is slightly different. Rather than pick up cards one by one, the player is given no option other than to pick up the entire pile. The next to play then starts a new one.

As players play their last cards, they drop out of play. If a player goes out by playing two cards, play continues as normal. If he has only one card left and goes out by beating the top card of the pile with it, the pile is turned face up and put to the side. The next player starts a new one by playing one card, and play continues as before.

CONCLUSION

A round ends when just one player is left with cards in his hand. The overall winner is the one who loses fewest of an agreed number of games. Alternatively, it is the player who has not lost a game when everyone else has lost at least one.

MUSTAMAIJA

This interesting game from Finland is related to several other Scandinavian beating games, in particular the Norwegian game of Spardame ('Spade Queen'), which it closely resembles. In both games, the aim is to avoid being the player left holding the Q♠ (known as 'Black Maria') when all the other players have successfully managed to get rid of their cards.

OBJECT

To avoid becoming 'Black Maria', or the loser who is left holding the Q♠.

THE DEAL

Each player is dealt five cards, one at a time. Those remaining are placed face down on the table as the stock.

PLAY

The player to the dealer's left starts the first round by playing between one to five cards of the same suit face up to the table. He may draw the necessary replacements from the stock. The cards may include the Q♠ if the other cards are spades.

Next, the dealer turns the top card of the stock face up to determine trumps. The usual convention is that Spades may not be trumps, so, if the turn-up is a Spade, the dealer places it in the middle of the stock and turns up the next card until another suit appears.

ATTACKERS AND DEFENDERS

The player to the dealer's left is designated as the initial attacker and the player to the attacker's left as the first defender. The latter must beat as many of the attacker's cards as possible by playing a higher card of the same suit, or, if the card is from a non-trump suit, playing a trump.

The attacker's beaten cards, and the ones used to beat them, are discarded and take no further part in the game. Any of the attacker's unbeaten cards must be picked up

Left: The Queen of Spades – a dreaded card in many betting games since the player left holding it loses the game. Known in Mustamaija as 'Black Maria', it can never be beaten, meaning that a defender is forced to pick it up and add it to his hand.

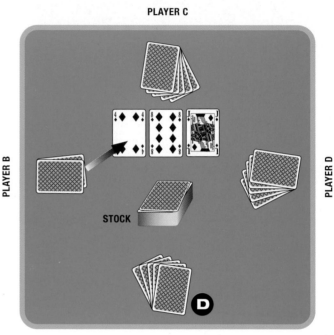

PLAYER C

PLAYER B

PLAYER D

STOCK

PLAYER A

Above: Player B (the player to the dealer's left) launches the first attack. Player C must beat each of the cards with higher Diamonds or trumps in order to defend successfully. If so, all the cards are discarded. Otherwise, Player C must pick up any unbeaten cards.

by the defender and taken into his hand. If the defender beats all of the attacker's cards, he becomes the next attacker. If not, he forfeits the chance to attack, which passes to the player to his left, who otherwise would have been the next defender. The Q♠ can neither beat nor be beaten by any other card, and must therefore always be taken up.

Once the stock is exhausted, a new rule states that an attacker cannot lead more cards than there are in a defender's hand. As players run out of cards, they drop out of play.

CONCLUSION

The last player left in, who invariably ends up holding the Q♠, is the loser, or 'Black Maria'.

KITUMAIJA

This unusual Finnish game is a cross between Durak and Mustamaija. The chief differences are that there are two classes of card, known as 'bound cards' and 'free cards', and permanent trump suits. Diamonds trump Spades and Hearts, but not Clubs, which are invulnerable.

OBJECT

To avoid being the player left with cards in hand, and thus the holder of the Q♠.

THE DEAL

Players are dealt five cards each, in packets of three and two. The dealer then deals a card face up to the table, to start the first spread. The remainder are placed face down to form the stock.

PLAY

Each player in turn, starting with the person to the dealer's left, must play as follows:

- If the topmost card of the spread is the Q♠, the next player must take it into hand, along with the top five cards of the spread (or as many as there are, if there are fewer than five), and end his turn.
- Otherwise, he must play a bound card – a higher card of the same suit – as the top card of the spread. If this top card is a Spade or a Heart, a Diamond can be played as trump, even if its player could have followed suit.

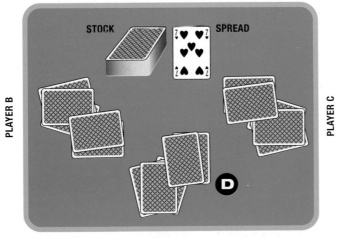

PLAYER A

Above: Five cards are dealt to each player, first in packets of three, then in packets of two. The next card is turned face up in the centre, to start what is known as the spread (i.e. the play pile). It is placed beside the stock.

You will need: 52 cards; no Jokers

Card ranking: Standard, except for the Q♠ (see under 'Play', below)

Players: Three to five

Ideal for: 10+

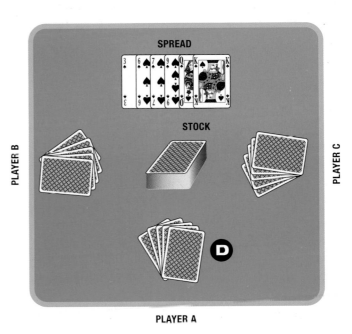

PLAYER A

Above: The next player must beat the King with an A♣, or a trump (Diamond) of any rank. If not, he must pick up the spread's first three cards.

- The bound card must be followed by a free card – this is a card of its player's choosing. The Q♠ can be played only as a free card, not as a bound one. Any player who cannot beat the top card has to pick up the first three cards of the spread and take them into hand.
- Until the stock run outs, the players replenish their hands from it, so they always have five cards in hand.

Once the stock has run out, no further free cards may be played. However, to give the Q♠ holder the chance to get rid of it, many players opt to ignore this rule and continue playing bound and free cards, as before. The alternative is to make an exception in the case of the Q♠. Players drop out as they run out of cards.

CONCLUSION

The last player left in, who invariably will be the player left holding the Q♠, is the loser.

HÖRRI

This game is the Finnish equivalent of Durak. Many Finnish card games are related to Russian ones, owing to the fact that Finland was a province of the Tsarist Empire up until the 1917 Revolution.

You will need: 52 cards; no Jokers
Card ranking: Standard, except for the Q♠, which has no rank
Players: Two to five
Ideal for: 14+

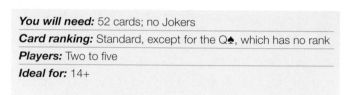

OBJECT

To avoid being the player left with cards in hand, and thus the holder of the Q♠.

THE DEAL

Instead of dealing cards as normal, the entire pack is placed face down in the centre of the table to form the stock. The dealer then takes the top eight cards of the stock and arranges them face up around it.

THE DRAW

Each player in turn draws a card from the stock. Diamonds trump Spades and Hearts, but not Clubs, which are invulnerable. If a Spade, Heart or Club is drawn, and the turn-up cards include a lower-ranking card of the same suit, the player takes all these cards into his hand. If there is no such card, the drawn card is replaced and the next player draws. If the next player draws a Diamond, and the turn-up cards include a lower-ranking Diamond or any Spade or Heart, all of these are added to the player's hand.

PLAYER C

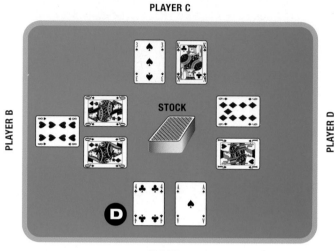

Above: Player B has drawn the 8♥. Since there are no lower Hearts among the turn-ups, the card is replaced and it is Player C's turn to draw.

Once the stock has been exhausted, the last player to take two cards adds any remaining turn-up cards to his hand. Naturally, the players end up with hands of varying length. Some may have no cards at all, in which case they have to sit out play.

PLAY

The player holding the 2♠ plays it face up to the table to start a spread of discards. Each player tries to lead a higher-ranking card of the same suit as the top card, or, if the top card is a Heart or Spade, trump it with a Diamond.

If unable or unwilling to play, the player concerned takes the bottom card of the spread and adds it to his hand. If a player 'completes' the spread – that is, plays a card that makes the number of cards the spread contains the same as the number of players – the spread is turned face down and a new one started.

PLAYER C

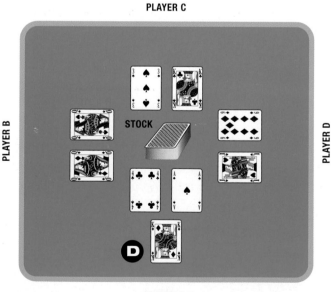

Above: Player A draws the K♦. It is higher than the 9♦ and, as Diamonds trump Spades and Hearts, he must also take the 3♠, the A♣ and the J♥.

CONCLUSION

The last player left in – who invariably will be holding the Q♠ – is the loser.

SKITGUBBE

This is a popular Swedish game, originally for three players. Play is divided into two phases. Skitgubbe means 'dirty old man' (in the sense of unwashed), and is the name given to the loser.

You will need: 52 cards

Card ranking: Standard

Players: Three

Ideal for: 14+

OBJECT

To collect, in the first phase of the game, cards that can be discarded as quickly as possible in the second phase.

THE DEAL

Each player is dealt three cards. The remainder are placed face down in a pile on the table to form the stock.

PLAY

This consists of tricks played by two players at a time, beginning with the two non-dealers. There is no need to follow suit – the highest card takes the trick. If the player who led wins the trick, he leads again with the same player; otherwise, the next trick is contested by the other two players, and so on. Cards from the trick are placed face-down in front of the player who wins them.

If the cards are equal, this is a *Stunza* (bounce). The cards are placed face up on the table, both players draw a card from the stock and the same player leads again. This continues until one of the players takes a trick.

PLAYER B

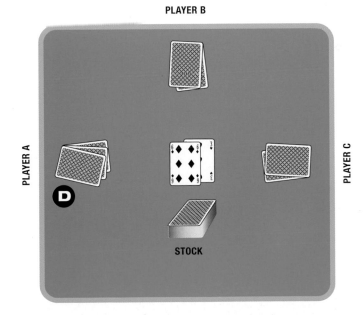

STOCK

PLAYER A

PLAYER C

Above: Player B lays the 3♥, but Player C tops this with the 6♦. Player C must place both cards face-down on the table next to him and lay a fresh card to Player A.

The trick winner takes all the cards that have been played (including those in the *Stunza*), turns them face down in front of himself and leads to the next trick.

Each player draws a card from the stock after playing. Rather than playing from hand, a player can opt to turn up the top card of the stock and play that instead.

Left: If two cards of the same rank, such as these two Kings, are played in the first phase of the game, this is known as a S*tunza*. The cards are placed face up on the table, and both players draw a card from the stock, beginning a new trick. The trick winner takes all the played cards, and begins a new trick.

Once the stock runs out, play carries on for as long as possible. Then, all three players use the cards they have won, together with any cards they may have left in hand, as their playing hands. The aim is to play out all one's cards. The player who drew the last card from the stock leads, its suit determining trumps. Now all three players play in turn, not two at a time as in phase one.

The leader may play a single card, or a sequence of two or more cards in the same suit. For example, the player concerned could elect to lead a Two and a Three or a Three, Four and Five, and so on, provided that whatever cards he decides to play are all of the same suit.

In order to take the trick, the cards that the opposing players play must be better – of the same suit but higher in rank – or, if a non-trump suit has been led, they must be a trump or trump sequence. A player may play trumps even if he is able to follow suit. The winner of the trick leads to the next.

A player who cannot play a better card picks up the last cards to be played. The player to the left then leads.

CONCLUSION

The last player left with cards in hand is the loser.

Shed

Also known as Karma and Palace, among other names, Shed's origins are a mystery. What is clear, however, is its international acceptance.

Object

To avoid being the last player left holding cards.

The Deal

The addition of two Jokers to the pack is optional for up to five players, but essential for six. The dealer deals three cards face down to each player. These are the down-cards. Three cards are then dealt face up – the up-cards – and finally three cards to hand. Any remaining cards are placed face down to form the stock.

Before play starts, each player has the option to exchange any of the cards in hand with the up-cards. No one may look at their down-cards until they are played.

Play and Conclusion

The first player to declare a Three in his hand leads. He plays any number of cards of the same rank face up to start the discard pile and then replenishes his hand from the stock to keep a minimum of three cards. Each player in clockwise turn must then play a card or cards of equal

You will need: 52 cards, with two Jokers added

Card ranking: Two (highest), then Ace down to Two again, since Twos rank both high and low

Players: Two to six

Ideal for: 10+

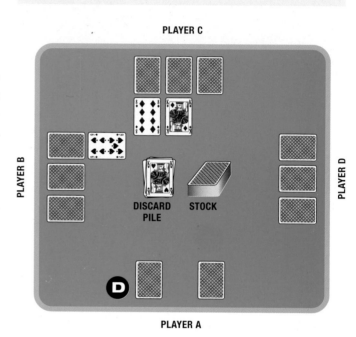

PLAYER C

PLAYER B

PLAYER D

DISCARD PILE

STOCK

D

PLAYER A

Above: Players B's up-card is not of equal rank or higher to Player A's K♥, so he must pick up the discard pile and revert to playing in hand.

or higher rank to beat the pile's top card. If a player cannot discard, he picks up the discard pile and the next player starts a new one.

A Joker may be played at any time, and simply reverses the direction of play. Twos rank high and low, so one or more may be played at any time – the next player in turn may play any other rank. Tens can be played on any card, in which case, the discard pile is removed from play and the same player gets another turn to start a new one. The discard pile is also removed from play if a set of four cards of the same rank is played.

As players' hands run out, they switch to playing from their up-cards. If a player is forced to pick up the discard pile, he reverts to playing from hand. Once the up-cards are played, the down-cards are played (blind) one at a time. If the flipped card does not beat the top card on the discard pile, the discard pile is picked up. As players run out of cards, they drop out of play.

The winner is the first to discard the last down card and the loser is the last left holding cards – 'the shed'.

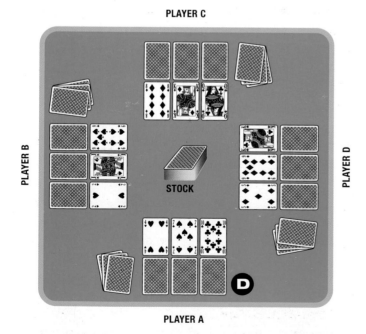

PLAYER C

PLAYER B

PLAYER D

STOCK

D

PLAYER A

Above: Three cards are dealt face down and three face up to each player. Three are then dealt to each player's hands and the remainder of the cards are placed in the centre to form the stock.

PASKAHOUSU

Verbal declarations and challenges are an integral part of play of this Finnish game. An ability to bluff successfully and a sharp card sense are essential qualities for would-be winners.

You will need: 52 cards

Card ranking: None

Players: Three or more, but ideally four or five

Ideal for: 14+

OBJECT

To bluff, and avoid being the last left holding cards.

THE DEAL

Each player receives five cards, and the remaining cards are placed face down to form the stock.

PLAY

Starting with the player to the dealer's left, each player can pass, play a card face down claiming it to be a Three (whether or not truthfully), or draw the top card from the stock and play it sight unseen, making the same claim. If everyone passes, the process starts again, although the first discard is now claimed to be a Four.

Declarations and Challenges

Each player in turn plays a card or sequence of cards face down to the discard pile, declaring them to be of equal or higher rank than that of the cards previously announced. This may or may not be true. However, before the next player plays, the most recent declaration can be challenged, in which case, the cards in question must be turned face up.

If the declaration was true, the challenger must add the whole discard pile to his hand. If not, the challenged player must pick up. In either case, play passes to the player to the left of the player who was challenged.

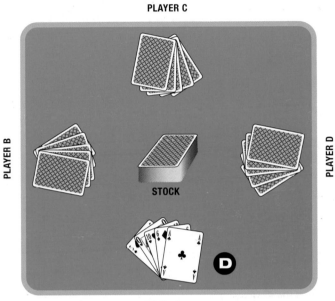

PLAYER C

PLAYER B

STOCK

PLAYER D

D

PLAYER A

Above: At the start of the game, Players B, C and D have all passed. Having no Three (the card required as an opening lay), Player A can either pass as well or he can play a card from his hand (or the top card of the stock, sight unseen), claiming it as a Three. It's then up to the remaining players to challenge or leave the declaration unchallenged.

Special Rules

- A Jack, Queen or King may not be declared unless the previous declaration was Eight or higher.
- An Ace may not be declared unless the previous call was one of the court cards – or the discard pile is empty.
- A Two may be called at any time, but the next play must be another Two.
- If Tens are called unchallenged, a new discard pile is started. If a Ten is played to an empty table, the next to play must pick it up and miss a turn.
- A player may opt to draw the top card of the stock and add it to his hand (instead of playing from hand).

Left: Jacks, Queens and Kings cannot be declared unless the previous declaration was Eight or higher.

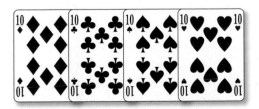

Left: If Tens are declared but unchallenged, the discard pile is moved out of play and a new one is started.

CONCLUSION

The game continues until all the players, bar one, are out of cards. That player is the loser.

CHEAT

Known as I Doubt It, as well as another cruder title in the USA, this children's game remains popular with young people. There are many versions. It is an ideal game for larger groups to play, and 'cheats' or those who wrongly accuse can be given forfeits or dares.

OBJECT

To be the first player to get rid of all his cards (using false calls where necessary), but without cheating on the final play. To disrupt others by spotting cheats and making accusations.

THE DEAL

All the cards are dealt out singly to the players (some may end up with one card more than others).

PLAY

The player to the dealer's left plays first, play going clockwise around the table. Each player in turn discards from one to four cards face down, calling out their rank

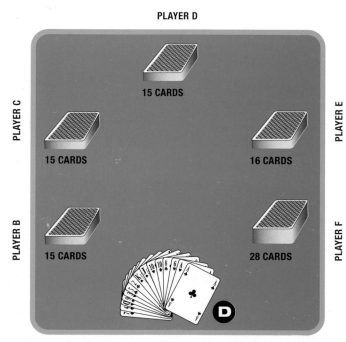

PLAYER D

PLAYER C

15 CARDS

PLAYER B

15 CARDS

15 CARDS

16 CARDS

28 CARDS

PLAYER E

PLAYER F

PLAYER A

Above: Player F has been caught cheating and has had to pick up all the cards previously laid. Player A can legitimately lay the two Aces or Tens face down, announcing them as such, or add a card of a different rank to one of these, announcing 'Three Aces', for example. The onus would then be on one of the other players to make a challenge.

You will need: 52 cards; no Jokers (two packs when more than five are playing)

Card ranking: None

Players: Two to 10

Ideal for: 7+

as they do so. The first to play calls 'Aces', the second 'Twos', the third 'Threes' and so on, up through the card ranks. After Tens come Jacks, followed by Queens and Kings, and then it is back to Aces again.

CHALLENGING

The cards a player puts out supposedly belong to the rank that they are declared to be. In practice, however, a player may lie – in fact, lying may be compulsory since you must play at least one card even when your hand does not contain any cards of the required rank.

If any player thinks that call and cards do not match, he can challenge play by calling 'Cheat'. The cards that the player who is being challenged played are then turned face up. If the challenge is false, the challenger picks up the discard pile and takes it into hand. He may also be given a forfeit. If any played card is not of the called rank, the challenge is correct and the person who played the cards picks up the pile and adds them to his hand. The cheat may also be given a forfeit. If there is no challenge, play continues.

The winner of a challenge is the next to play, calling the next rank in sequence, although in some versions of the game, he can choose whichever rank he likes to call.

VARIANTS

Other versions include making the sequence of ranks that have to be played run downwards (for example, Aces, Kings, Queens, Jacks etc.), and allowing players to play, or claim to play, the next rank above or the next rank below the one called by the preceding player.

CONCLUSION

The first player to get rid of all his cards and defeat a challenge arising from his final play wins the game. If there is a successful challenge, he must pick up the pile and play continues until there is a winner.

VERISH' NE VERISH'

A cross between Cheat and Old Maid, another children's game, this Russian offering is slightly more complicated, but well worth the effort. The name itself translates as 'Trust, Don't Trust' or, more colloquially, as 'Believe It Or Not'.

You wil need:	52-card deck with Twos to Sixes removed
Card ranking:	None
Players:	Up to six
Ideal for:	7+

OBJECT

To avoid, through bluffs, becoming the last with cards.

THE DEAL

For two to three players, use a 32-card pack; for four to six players, use a standard 52-card pack. After the cards have been shuffled, one card is drawn at random and put face down to the side, after which the rest are dealt singly, face down to all the players in clockwise rotation.

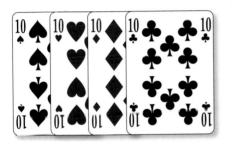

Left: A player starting a new round is allowed to discard any sets of four cards he has been dealt, such as these four Tens.

PLAY

A game consists of several rounds and each round is made up of what are termed moves. It is generally played by up to six players. The player to the dealer's left makes the first move by playing up to four cards face down to the table and declaring their rank – although this declaration need not necessarily be true.

The next player has two options. He may say '*Verish*' ('I trust you'), or nothing, because trust is assumed, in which case he plays, face down, the same number of cards as the previous player and calls the same rank (truthfully or not), awaiting whether the next player will challenge him or not. Or, he may decide to challenge the previous player, and say instead '*Ne Verish*' ('I don't trust you'), and turn the previously played cards face up to discover the truth.

If the cards rank as declared, the unsuccessful challenger has to pick up all the cards so far played in the game. If, on the other hand, the challenge is correct, the player who was challenged must pick up the cards and take them into hand.

This ends the round, the next being started by the player to the left of the penalized player (this should be the challenger himself, if he was correct). Before play starts, that player is entitled to discard any set of four cards of the same rank, showing them to the others before setting them aside. This obviously decreases the number of cards in play.

As play continues, more and more sets of four cards are eliminated. However, because one card is removed from the pack before the deal, the other three cards of this rank necessarily remain in play until the end of the game.

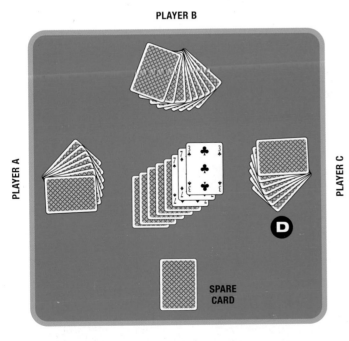

PLAYER B

PLAYER A

PLAYER C

SPARE CARD

Above: Player C, the third to play, laid down three cards, claiming them to be three Sevens, but Player B challenged, saying '*Ne Verish*'. Player C must expose the cards, revealing that one is a Three, and pick up all the cards on the table. A new round then begins.

CONCLUSION

The eventual loser is the player who is left holding one or more of the initially discarded ranked cards, while the other players have managed to get rid of all their cards successfully.

8 | RUMMY GAMES

THERE ARE MANY DIFFERENT GAMES OF THIS TYPE, THE ORIGINS OF WHICH SEEM TO BE CHINESE. INDEED, THEY WERE UNKNOWN IN THE WEST UNTIL THE EARLY 20TH CENTURY. THEY ARE KNOWN TECHNICALLY AS DRAW-AND-DISCARD GAMES, IN WHICH THE OBJECTIVE IS TO COLLECT MATCHING CARDS, EITHER OF THE SAME RANK OR SEQUENCES IN A SUIT, AND MELD THEM INTO SETS, WHICH ARE THEN DISCARDED AND COUNTED UP AT THE END OF THE GAME.

In basic rummy games, such as Rummy itself, the aim is simple – to meld an entire hand into groups and then to discard the melds as quickly as possible. This sounds easy enough, but, as is often the case, there can be complications.

Loba (meaning 'she-wolf'), a South American version of Rummy much played in Argentina, can be either a positive or a negative game. In the former, Loba de Más, players score points for the melds they make and lose points for cards remaining in hand at the end of play. The objective is to score as many points as possible. In the latter, Loba de Menos, points are scored for cards in hand when play ends, but the objective is to score as few points as possible. Melds do not score.

In Three Thirteen, an American Rummy game, the number of cards dealt to each player differs from round to round, and there is a different wild card in each round. The number of cards dealt determines which card is the wild card.

What is termed Contract Rummy is played in much the same way as basic Rummy, the fundamental difference being that, in each round, the players' melds have to conform to a specific contract. Each player must also collect a particular combination of groups and sequences of cards before they can start to meld. The contract becomes harder with successive deals.

Contract Rummy is less a single game than a protracted contest: a typical game consists of seven deals.

Above: Tiles for Mahjong, a game that originated in China. The play in Rummy closely resembles that of the Chinese game, and probably derives from it.

Rummy

Straight Rummy, as it is sometimes called, first appeared in the early 1900s in the USA, where it also went under other names, such as Coon Can, Khun Khan and Colonel. How it originated is uncertain, though some think that it was derived from a Mexican game called Conquian, the earliest known Rummy game in the Western world, or from Rum Poker.

Object

To be the first to get rid of all one's cards by melding, laying off and discarding cards.

Melds, Lay Offs and Discards

There are two types of meld – sequences (runs) and groups (sets or books). Three or more cards of the same suit in consecutive order make up a sequence; a group is three or four cards of the same rank. Laying off means adding a card or cards to a meld you have played face up to the table. Players must discard one card onto the discard pile after each turn. No player may add to another's meld until he has laid down one of his own.

The Deal

The first dealer is chosen at random, the deal then passing to the left. If there are two players, each receives 10 cards, three or four get seven and more than four players receive six cards. The cards are dealt singly; then a

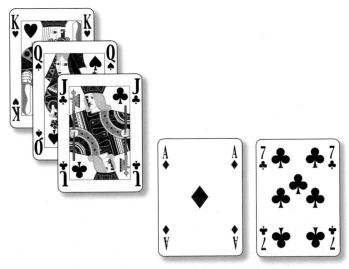

Above: The court cards score 10 points each, the Ace scores one point and the Seven scores its face value. These scores are added to the winner's total.

You will need: 52 cards; scorecards

Card ranking: See under 'Scoring', below

Players: Two to six, but best played with four

Ideal for: 7+

Left: In this hand, the four Fours make up a group and the three court cards form a sequence in Diamonds.

card is turned face up to start the discard pile and the remaining cards put face down beside it to form the stock. Thorough shuffling is essential before each deal.

Play

The player to the dealer's left leads. Each player starts by drawing a card from the top of the stock, or the top card of the discard pile. Each can then play a meld, or lay off. Only one meld may be played per turn. The top card picked up from the discard pile cannot be discarded, but one drawn from the stock can. If the stock runs out, the discard pile is turned face down to form a new stock.

Scoring

In the version of Rummy given here, after a player goes out the remaining players add up the value of any cards that are not melded or that have not been declared and shown. Court cards are worth 10 points each, Aces one point and number cards face value. The cumulative total is added to the winner's score. In some versions, points count against players instead, one variation allowing them to wipe their score by collecting a sequence of seven cards of the same suit. The game should be played to a fixed number of deals or to a target score.

Conclusion

Play comes to an end when one player gets rid of all his cards. The winner is the player with the highest score.

RUMMY VARIANTS

Over time, many modifications have been made to the basic rules and structure of Rummy, so exactly which rules are being played should always be agreed before the start of the first deal. Some games, for instance, allow multiple melds; in others a player who has yet to meld or lay off wins a double score if he succeeds in going out in one turn. This is 'going rummy'.

HOUSE RULES

Practically every player favours a different set of house rules, the majority of which are optional. Some prefer, for instance, that no cards can be laid off on other players' melds unless the player wishing to do so has already laid down at least one meld of his own. In some games, though, a player may lay off cards only to his own or his partner's melds, while others allow cards to be laid off to any meld on the table.

ACE HIGH OR LOW

Whether Aces are played high or low is a perennial debate. In the standard game of Rummy, they are low – so Ace, Two, Three is a valid sequence, while Queen, King, Ace is not. In some games, however, Aces are allowed to count as either, and are worth 11 points each in consequence. Such games are referred to as Round-the-Corner Rummy: this is because, if Aces are high, a sequence may 'turn the corner', as in High-Low Rummy.

Left: Examples of melds when the Ace counts high and low. Some variations allow only one of these options, others both.

STOCK-PILE VARIATIONS

Other variations specify how players can go out, what happens when the stock is exhausted, and how a hand is scored. In Discard Rummy, a player has to discard his last card – it cannot form part of a meld or be laid off. Alternatively, the discard pile is shuffled before being used as the new stock and limits may be placed on how many times this can happen.

Right: A classic family game, Rummy has almost as many house rules as there are homes! All kinds of variations have sprung up, so players choose for themselves the conventions that fit them best.

BLOCK RUMMY

In Block Rummy, the discard pile is not reused at all. Assuming no one wants to pick up the top card of the discard pile, the hand ends once the stock is exhausted. Players score the value of the cards in hand, the winner being the player with the fewest points.

BOATHOUSE RUM AND CALL RUMMY

Both these variants are played much like basic Rummy, but with several important differences. In Boathouse Rum, a player drawing the turn-up from the discard pile must also draw the top card of the stock, or a second turn-up. Either way, he draws two cards. Cards may not be laid off and nobody can meld until one player goes rummy. At that point, the other players lay down as many melds as they can and the hand is then scored in the usual manner.

Call Rummy means just that. If any player discards a card that could be laid off against a meld, any other player can call out 'Rummy', pick up the discard, lay it off himself and replace it with one from his own hand. If two or more players make the call simultaneously, the one who is next in turn to play wins the call.

SKIP RUMMY AND WILD-CARD RUMMY

Both of these versions are played in much the same way as basic Rummy. In Skip Rummy, the principle difference is that sequences cannot be melded, only groups. In addition, once a player has laid down a meld, he is allowed to lay off the fourth card of a rank to his own or to any other player's three cards of the same rank. A player who is left with a pair in hand can go out without discarding as soon as he draws a third card of the same rank. Play ends when one player goes out, or when the number of cards in the stock equals the number of players. The discard pile is not reused.

In Wild-Card Rummy, Twos and Jokers – it is a further option whether the latter are played – are wild. They score 25 points each. Players can steal a wild card from any meld on the table provided that they can replace it with the card it represents, but no one may meld until one player has gone rummy. Scoring works in the normal way.

Right: In this wild-card version of Rummy, the 2♥ and Joker are wild cards so can count as anything. Here they represent Sevens, thus completing a winning meld.

Far right: In this One-Meld Rummy game, having picked up the Q♣, this player completes a second meld and wins the game.

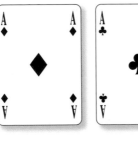

KRAMBAMBULI

Other Rummy games adopting the same principle include Krambambuli, which hails from Germany. In this two- to three-player game, one of the options open to a player is to steal cards from another player's melds. You can do this provided that the theft does not invalidate the meld, that you can combine it with at least two cards from your own hand to make a new meld and that you do not steal more than one card a turn. The lowest score wins.

ONE-MELD AND TWO-MELD RUMMY

The difference between these variants lies in the way players can go out in a hand. In the former, a player can go out only by going rummy, that is, by melding every card in hand at once, with or without the benefit of the discard. The player concerned scores the value of the meld multiplied by the number of players.

In Two-Meld Rummy, going rummy is forbidden. Any player able to do so must keep a meld in reserve to be laid down on his next turn.

Left and Below: In Krambambuli, melds are more or less communal property. In the situation here, with a meld of four Aces on the table, a player holding the hand shown below could pick up the A♠ from the table to make a sequence (Ace, Two, Three).

GIN RUMMY

Often referred to affectionately simply as Gin, its countless aficionados consider this to be the only form of Rummy worth playing. Best as a two-player game, it is far harder to master than it appears. When played well, it is a fast, exciting game, some players being expert enough to bring a hand to an end after only six or so draws.

You will need: 52 cards; scorecards	
Card ranking: None	
Players: Two	
Ideal for: 10+	

TWO-PLAYER GIN

OBJECT

To end up with a hand in which most or all of the cards can be melded into groups – that is, three or more cards of the same rank – and sequences, which must consist of three or more cards in suit and sequence. Numerals count at face value, court cards 10 each and Aces one.

THE DEAL

In Two-Player Gin Rummy, each player receives 10 cards, dealt singly. After the deal, the next card is turned up to start the discard pile and the remaining cards are placed face down to form the stock.

PLAY

The non-dealing player always plays first. He must start by taking the turn-up or passing, in which case the dealer has the same option. If both players pass, the non-dealing player must take the top card of the stock. Subsequently, each player can take a card from either pile. At the end of his turn, each must discard a card face up on to the discard pile. If a player opts to take the turn-up, this cannot be discarded in the same turn.

KNOCKING

Either player can end play by 'knocking' – that is discarding one card face down to the discard pile and exposing the rest of the hand, arranged as far as possible into sequences and groups. For the knock to be valid, any deadwood (the value of unmatched cards) must not be worth more than 10 points. Knocking with no deadwood

Right: Player A has here knocked and laid down his hand. With just one unmatched card (the Ace, counting for one point), this hand scores 13 points. Player B has unmatched cards worth 14 points. Had the hands been the other way round, Player B would have scored 13 points plus a bonus of 10 for what is known as the undercut.

in hand is called 'going gin' and is worth an extra bonus. Play also stops if the stock is down to two cards and the player who took the third-to-last card discards without knocking. In this case, there is no score and the same dealer deals again. Once a player has knocked, the opposing player shows his cards. Provided that the knocker did not go gin, the opposing player can lay off unmatched cards by extending the melds laid down by the knocker. The reverse, however, is not allowed – the knocker is never permitted to lay off unmatched cards.

SCORING

Each court card is worth 10 points and Aces one, while the number cards count at face value. At the end of the game, both players count the values of their unmatched cards. If the knocker's count is higher than that of his opponent, he scores the difference between the two counts, plus a bonus of 20 points if he went gin, plus the opponent's count in unmatched cards, if any.

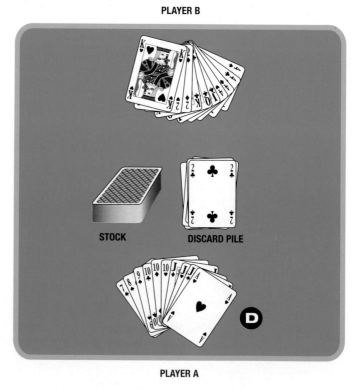

PLAYER B

STOCK   DISCARD PILE

PLAYER A

If the knocker's count is lower than that of his opponent, or if the counts are equal, the opposing player scores the difference between the two, plus a 10-point bonus for what is termed the 'undercut'.

Melds

Two types of meld (card combination) are used in Gin Rummy:

- A group or set – three or more cards of the same rank.
- A sequence or run – three or more cards of the same suit in consecutive order.

A card can be used only in one combination at a time. It is against the rules of the game to try to use the same card as part of a group and a sequence.

Conclusion

A player must reach a cumulative score of 100 points or more to win the game. Both players also receive a bonus 20 points for each hand they won, and the winner adds an extra bonus of a further 100 points for the game – 200 if the losing player failed to score at all. After all the points have been totalled, the player with the lower score pays the winner an amount related to the difference between the two scores, which is doubled if the loser failed to win a single hand.

PLAYER B

PLAYER A

Above: Had Player A not gone gin, Player B could have laid off the 6♠ on Player A's sequence and the J♠ on the group. As it is, no laying off is permitted, so Player A will score 19 points for Player B's unmatched cards plus another 20 points for going gin.

PLAYER B

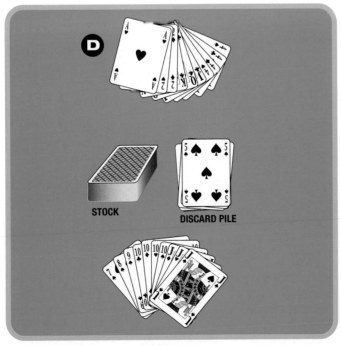

PLAYER A

THREE- AND FOUR-PLAYER GIN

If three players are playing, the dealer deals to the other two players and then sits out the hand, with the loser of the hand dealing the next. There is also a three-player variant called Jersey Gin, in which the winner scores the difference between his hand and that of each opponent.

Four can play as two partnerships, each player in one team playing a separate game with one of the opposing pair. Players alternate opponents from hand to hand, but stay in the same partnerships throughout the game.

If both partners win at the end of a hand, they score their combined total of points. If only one player from a partnership wins, the partnership with the higher total scores the difference. To win the game, a partnership needs to reach a cumulative total of 125 points or more.

Left: In this game Player A has melded every card before knocking and laying down his hand. Player B is still waiting for a Two. Although the difference between unmatched cards is only five points, Player A scores a bonus of 20 points for going gin.

LOBA

This Argentinian game can be played negatively (Loba de Menos), when the aim is to score as few points as possible, and positively (Loba de Más), when it is to score high. Both versions are played in much the same way, except in Loba de Más, Twos can be used as natural Twos or wild cards.

OBJECT

To be the first player to go out in the negative game, or the highest-scoring player in the positive version.

THE DEAL

Each player receives nine cards (11 in the positive version), the next being turned to start the discard pile. The remainder form the stock.

PLAY

Each player draws the top card of the discard pile or the top card of the stock. A card can be drawn from the former only if played immediately. In the positive game, the whole of the discard pile must be taken.

Melding follows. No player may add to another's meld until he has laid down one of his own. In Loba de Más (the positive game), players may add only to their own melds. Finally, a card is discarded face up. Jokers may be discarded only if they are the last cards held.

SCORING

In the negative game, the first to go out scores nothing, the other(s) scoring penalty points. Jokers, Aces and the court cards score 10 points each, number cards face value. Players scoring more than 101 points must drop out unless they elect to buy back in by paying a stake in chips into the pot. This is allowed twice.

> ### MELDS
>
> There are two types of meld (card combination) that are allowed in Loba:
>
> - A *Pierna* – three or more cards of the same rank, but of different suits.
> - An *Escalera* – three or more cards of the same suit in sequence.
>
> Jokers cannot be used in *Piernas*, and *Escaleras* can contain only one. In the positive game, *Escaleras* can contain any number of wild cards, although these cannot all be Jokers.

You will need: Two 52-card decks; four Jokers; scorecards; gambling chips/counters
Card ranking: See under 'Scoring', below
Players: Two to five
Ideal for: 10+

In the positive game, melds score positive points, cards in hand negative ones. An Ace in a meld scores three points if high, one point if low, Kings to Eights two and Sevens to Threes score one. Jokers and Twos are worth three if substituting for Aces to Eights, otherwise one. The negative values are three for Aces, Jokers and Twos, two for Kings to Eights and one for Sevens to Threes.

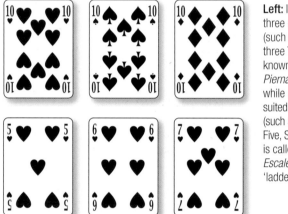

Left: In Loba, three of a kind (such as the three Tens) is known as a *Pierna*, or 'leg', while a same-suited sequence (such as the Five, Six, Seven) is called an *Escalera*, or 'ladder'.

CONCLUSION

A round ends when a player gets rid of all his cards. In Loba de Menos, the game is won when all other players have exceeded 101 points and are prohibited from buying their way back in again, and in Loba de Más when a player reaches 150 or more positive points. The winner takes the pot.

Above: An *Escalera* in Loba de Más can contain any number of wild cards, but they cannot all be Jokers. Here, the Jokers represent the 6♥ and 7♥.

THIRTY-ONE

Also known as Scat and Blitz, this is a straightforward draw-and-discard game. One of the oldest known gambling games, it has been popular in Europe since the 15th century.

You will need: 52 cards; gambling chips/counters

Card ranking: See under 'Scoring', below

Players: Two to nine, although probably best with three

Ideal for: 7+

OBJECT

To collect cards of the same suit totalling 31 points, or as near 31 as possible.

THE DEAL

The first dealer is chosen at random. After the deal of three cards to each player, the remaining cards are stacked face down to form the stock, the top card being turned up and placed separately to start a discard pile.

Left: An example of the highest possible hand in Thirty-One: two court cards and an Ace of the same suit, together worth 31 points.

PLAY

The normal practice is to start off with three chips each and all the players deciding which will be their particular points suit. The maximum hand value possible is 31, which would mean holding the Ace and two court cards of the same suit. If a player holds cards of three different suits, the value of the hand is that of

Above: Here, the A♦, 7♠, 3♥, which scores 11 for the Ace but nothing for the other two cards, is beaten by the J♠, Q♠, K♠ (scoring 30).

the highest card. Play rotates to the left. Each player in turn draws the top card from the discard pile or the stock and throws away a single card on to the discard pile. If the top discard is taken, it cannot be thrown away in the same turn, but a card drawn from the stock can be.

SCORING

Aces are worth 11 points, court cards 10 points each and number cards their face value. Winning the game depends on the number of lives lost. (In variations of the game a player scores $30\frac{1}{2}$ points for three of a kind).

Left: This player may hold an Ace and two court cards, but the hand's value is only 11 points, corresponding to the Ace, the highest-ranked card of the three.

CONCLUSION

The game continues until a player succeeds in scoring 31 points, in which case the cards are shown immediately. All the other players lose a life and pay a chip into the pool. The alternative is to knock before reaching 31 points. The knocker stops playing, the others getting one last chance to draw and discard. Then all the players show their hands. The player with the lowest hand value loses a life. If scores are tied, the knocker is safe, but the other player or players involved also lose a life each.

If the knocker is the loser, which can happen because he scores the lowest, or because another player declares 31 after the knock, he forfeits two lives. Players who have lost three lives can play on, but if they lose again, they are out of the game. The last player left in wins.

THREE THIRTEEN

This is Rummy with a difference. In each of its 11 rounds, there is a different wild card, while a differing number of cards, three to 13, is dealt to each player. The number of cards determines which is the wild card. At the end of a round, players arrange as many of their cards as they can into groups, and any cards left over score penalties.

OBJECT

To form the cards in hand into groups, preferably of high-scoring cards. Groups consist of three or more cards of the same rank, or consecutive sequences of three or more cards in the same suit.

WILD CARDS

There are different wild cards in each round: Threes in the first, Fours in the second and so on up to Kings. Aces, which are ranked low in this game, are never wild cards. A wild card can stand in for any other card – it can even be used to make up a complete group.

THE DEAL

The first dealer is chosen at random, after which the deal passes to the left after each round. In the first of these, three cards are dealt to each player, in the second four,

and so on up to the final round, when, instead of 11 cards, 13 are dealt. The remaining cards are placed face down on the table to form the stock, the top card being turned up and put beside it to start a discard pile.

PLAY

The player to the dealer's left starts and play progresses clockwise around the table. Each player draws a card from the top of the stock or the discard pile and discards a card face up on to the latter. Players arrange as many cards as they can into groups, with penalty points being scored for any unmatched ones. A player can announce that he is out (has matched all his cards into groups) only when discarding, and the other players each get one more turn before the round ends and the scores are calculated.

SCORING

Any unmatched card counts against players. Aces score a point, Tens and the court cards 10 points and other number cards their face value.

You will need: 52-card deck for two players; two 52-card decks for three or more; scorecards

Card ranking: See under 'Scoring', below

Players: Two or more players

Ideal for: 7+

PLAYER C

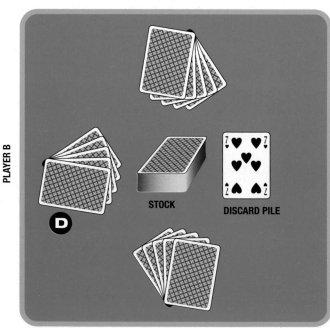

PLAYER B

STOCK

DISCARD PILE

D

PLAYER A

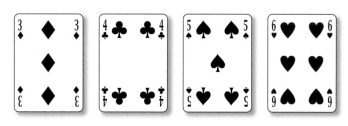

Left: As well as wild cards changing in each round, so too does the number of cards dealt. It starts at three and increases by one at a time, until 13 cards are dealt in the 11th round. In the third round, players receive five cards, as here.

Above: Wild cards in Three Thirteen change round by round, ascending one rank after each deal. The cards shown here, therefore, are possible examples of wild cards in each of the first four rounds of the game.

CONCLUSION

The player who has the lowest cumulative score at the end of the game is the winner.

CONQUIAN

Dating from the 1880s, this two-player game is thought to have originated in Mexico. It is considered by some to be the ancestor of all subsequent Rummy games devised in the West, although others say their origin is Chinese.

You will need: 40 cards (52-card deck with Eights, Nines and Tens removed)

Card ranking: Ace, lowest, up to Seven and then Jack, Queen and King (highest)

Players: Two

Ideal for: 7+

OBJECT

To be the first player to go out by melding 11 cards – that is, the 10 cards that are being held, plus the top card of the stock.

THE DEAL

Each player gets 10 cards dealt singly, the remainder being placed face down to form the stock.

MELDS

There are two types of meld (card combination) in Conquian:

- A group or short – three or four cards of the same rank.
- A sequence or straight – three to eight consecutive cards of the same suit.

During play, both players are allowed to rearrange their melds to create new ones, provided that their existing melds still contain the minimum three cards they need to be valid. Melds always have to include a turn-up from the stock. They also must be kept entirely separate. It is against the rules for a player to lay off cards on the other's melds.

PLAY AND CONCLUSION

The non-dealer starts by turning up the top card of the stock and then exercises one of two options. The turn-up must be melded immediately with at least two cards held in hand, after which another card must be discarded face up to serve as the next turn-up. Otherwise the player must pass, after which the dealer must decide whether to do the same or meld with the turn-up.

If he chooses to pass, a new turn-up is drawn from the stock and the process begins again. If a player declines to play a turn-up that could be added to an existing meld, the opposing player can force the meld to be made. A shrewd tactician can take advantage of this to destroy the opposing player's position.

Play continues until a player goes out by melding the turn-up with all 10 cards held in hand. It also stops when the stock runs out. If neither player can make the final meld, the game is a draw and the stakes for the next one are doubled.

PLAYER B

NON-DEALER

STOCK

TURN-UP CARD

D

PLAYER A

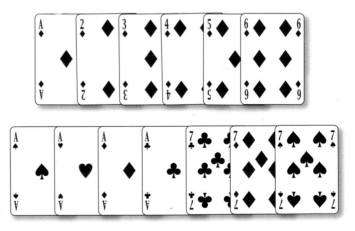

Above: Examples of melds in Conquian: first a sequence of six Diamonds; second, a group of Aces followed by a group of Sevens.

Left: Ten cards have been dealt to each player and, having turned up the Q♦, the non-dealer can pick it up if he is able to meld it with two cards in his hand. Otherwise, he must pass, allowing the dealer the opportunity to meld or pass. If the dealer also passes, a new turn-up card is drawn from the stock.

CONTRACT RUMMY

The oldest known game of this type is called Zioncheck, which dates from the 1930s. Many other variants, such as Hollywood Rummy, Joker Rummy and Shanghai Rummy, have been devised since then. In each game, players contract to make certain melds, dictated by which deal is in progress. Contracts get harder from round to round.

OBJECT

To make the required contract in a given round and end up, after seven deals, with the lowest score.

THE DEAL

There are seven deals in total. In the first three rounds, players receive 10 cards each, and then from the fourth round onwards, 12 cards. The first dealer is chosen at random, after which the deal passes to the left after each round. The deal is also clockwise, each player receiving one card at a time. The remaining cards are placed face down on the table to form the stock pile, the top card of which is turned face up and put alongside to start the discard pile. If the stock is exhausted before any player goes out, the convention is to turn the discard pile down, shuffle it, and use it as a replacement stock pile.

You will need: Two decks of 52 cards with single Joker for three to four players; three packs of 52 cards plus two Jokers for five to eight players; scorecards

Card ranking: Standard, Aces low or high; Jokers serve as wild cards; Twos can also count as wild cards

Players: Three to eight players

Ideal for: 14+

CONTRACTS

The contracts specifying which melds (card combinations) have to be laid down by each player differ in each of the seven rounds, as follows:

- First round – two groups of three cards.
- Second round – a group of three and a sequence of four.
- Third round – two groups of four.
- Fourth round – three groups of three.
- Fifth round – two groups of three cards and one sequence of four.
- Sixth round – one group of three and two sequences of four.
- Seventh round – three sequences of four.

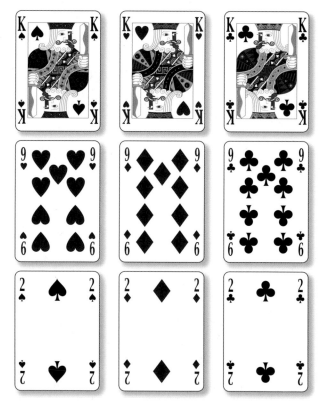

Above: An example of the melds required in the final round of Contract Rummy, when three sequences of four cards have to be laid down. Note that the third sequence actually contains five cards, since the 'discard' must be played in addition to the cards in hand in order to go out.

Above: In the fourth round of Contract Rummy, the card combinations needed are three groups (that is, cards of the same rank) of three. The groups shown here are of Kings, Nines and Twos.

PLAY

The player to the dealer's left plays first. Each player in turn starts by taking the top discard or drawing the top card of the stock. A player deciding to do the latter must wait until the others have had a chance to indicate whether they want to take the discard. A player does this by simply saying 'May I?' If more than one player makes the call, the discard goes to the next to play. Taking the discard like this means drawing an extra card from the stock as a penalty.

The first melds are then laid down. This can be done only once per round, although this does not necessarily have to be during the initial play. The melds must be the ones required by that round's contract (see box left).

Once players have melded, they are free to begin laying off the cards remaining in hand by adding cards to each other's melds, although this process cannot start until the turn after the initial meld has been laid. It is now within the rules to extend sequences, the longest possible one being 14 cards, with an Ace (one low and one high) at either end. To extend a group, players add more cards of equal rank to it.

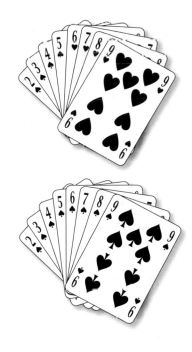

Right: This sequence of cards would be legal because the two four-card sequences within it are in a different suit.

Right: This sequence of cards in the same suit needs a gap between the Five and Six to be legal. Only one of the four-card sequences within it is valid.

SCORING

The first player to go out wins the round with a score of zero. The others score penalty points for the cards left in hand. Aces and Jokers score 15 points, the court cards 10 points each and the number cards are worth their face values. The scoring is cumulative, the player with the lowest score at the end of the final round winning the game.

PLAYER B

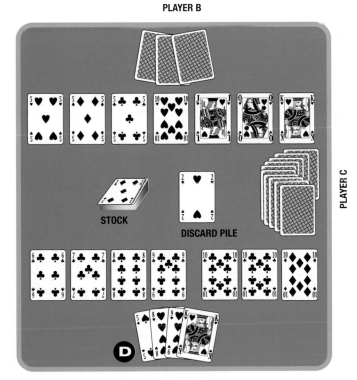

PLAYER A

Above: Players A and B have both laid down the required melds for the second round (a group of three and a sequence of four). Player A has picked up the 5♠ from the stack, which can be laid off on to Player B's group of Fives. Similarly, his 8♥ and 9♥ can be added to Player B's sequence, but the K♥ cannot be laid.

CONCLUSION

Play ends after the seventh deal, final scores then being calculated.

PUSH

This is the partnership version of Contract Rummy. Although it is played in much the same way, there are differences, notably in the way cards are drawn and discarded.

You will need: Two 52-card decks; four Jokers; scorecards
Card ranking: Standard, Aces high and low; Jokers and Twos are wild cards
Players: Four, in partnerships of two
Ideal for: 14+

OBJECT

To make, as a partnership, the required contract for each deal. The aim during the game is to get rid of all wild cards and valuable cards from your hand during play so that you do not accrue lots of penalty points if you lose the round. The partnership with the lowest number of penalty points at the end of the final round is the winner.

THE DEAL

In each deal there is a minimum requirement for each player's initial meld. There are five rounds: in the first, six cards are dealt to each player and so on until a final deal of 10 cards. The first dealer is chosen at random, after which the turn to deal passes to the left. Once the cards have been dealt, the next card is turned face up to start the discard pile and the remaining cards placed face down

to form the stock. If the first face-up card is a wild card (a Two or a Joker), the dealer will bury it in the stock pile and turn up a replacement card to start the discard pile.

CONTRACTS, MELDS AND WILD CARDS

The contracts specifying which melds (card combinations) have to be laid down by each player differ in each round as follows:

- First round – two groups of three equally ranking cards.
- Second round – one group of three cards and one sequence of four consecutive cards of the same suit.
- Third round – two sequences of four cards.
- Fourth round – three groups of three.
- Fifth round – two sequences of five.

Since two packs of cards are used, there are two of each card, which is why a group cannot contain two identical cards of the same suit. However, it is permissible to meld two groups of the same rank – an 8♣, 8♥ and 8♠ and an 8♥, 8♠ and 8♦, for instance, would be legal.

A sequence consists of three or more cards of the same suit in consecutive order. Aces can be either high or low, but not both at the same time. Once melded, sequences cannot be split up or joined together, but only extended by players laying off cards.

As wild cards, Twos and Jokers can be used to represent any card in any group or sequence. If a meld consists entirely of wild cards or has only one natural card in it, its player must state whether it is meant to be a group or a sequence. If the latter, what each card represents has to be specified, but, in the case of a group, it is necessary only to state the rank.

Below: In Push, the melds that are required change in each of the five rounds, examples being shown here.

ROUND 1

ROUND 2

ROUND 3

ROUND 4

ROUND 5

PLAY

The player to the dealer's left plays first, play continuing clockwise around the table. Each turn consists of three elements: drawing, melding and discarding.

DRAWING

As far as drawing is concerned, there are two options. If a player wants the top card of the discard pile, he may take it and add it to his hand. If a player does not want the top card, he can take a face-down card off the top of the undealt stock cards. The way this is done gives the game its name. The player takes a card from the stock, places it on the top card of the discard pile and then 'pushes' these two cards to the opposing player to the left, who must take these cards into hand. The first player then draws the next card from the stock pile. Because of the pushing, players can sometimes accumulate quite a large number of cards in their hands.

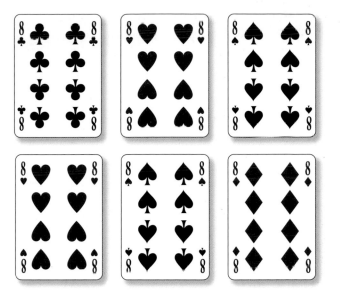

Above: Because two packs of cards are used in Push, it is possible to have two groups of the same rank, as shown here.

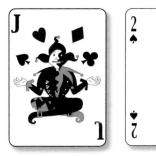

Left: If a wild card is turned up after the deal, it is buried in the stock and the dealer turns up a replacement.

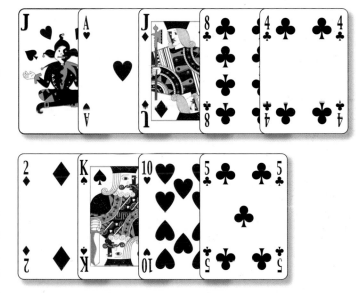

MELDING AND DISCARDING

Having drawn, players have the opportunity to lay their first melds face up on the table. Not only must these meet the terms of the contract for the round, but both players in a partnership must meld individually before they can go on to lay down further melds or lay off cards to any meld already on the table made by themselves or by their opponents.

If a player holds a card that is represented by a Joker in any meld, he may exchange it, as long as the Joker can be laid off on to another meld immediately, or used as part of a new one. It cannot be taken into hand. Players end their turns by discarding a card on to the discard pile.

SCORING

The losing partnership counts the value of the cards that both of them are still holding. Each Two or Joker counts for 20 penalty points, each Ace 15, each of the court cards and Tens 10 and the remaining cards five points each. Scoring is cumulative from round to round.

Above: A partnership left holding these cards would lose 100 points: 20 each for the Joker and Two, 15 for the Ace, 10 for the King, Jack and Ten, and five each for the Eight, Five and Four.

CONCLUSION

Play continues until a player succeeds in going out by getting rid of all the cards in hand. This involves melding or laying off the entire hand, or melding all bar one of the cards, which is then the last card to be discarded. It is at this point of the game that the penalty points are counted. The successful player and his partner score nothing – even though that partner will have cards remaining in hand.

KALUKI

Another version of Rummy with a difference, Kaluki, or Kalookie, is always played with a double pack, plus four Jokers as wild cards. The exact rules of play differ from place to place, but the ones detailed below are typical.

You will need: Two 52-card decks; four Jokers; gambling chips/counters
Card ranking: Standard, Aces high and low; Jokers are wild
Players: Two to five
Ideal for: 14+

OBJECT

To combine all cards in hand into groups and sequences. Stakes are agreed beforehand. The call-up is the amount the losers pay to the winner of each hand, while a kaluki is paid to a player who melds all 13 cards simultaneously. An initial stake is paid into the pool. Players may decide to set the stakes as follows: one unit (chip) for a call-up; two for a kaluki; three for the initial stake and five for a buy-in (see below under 'Scoring and Conclusion').

THE DEAL

The dealer shuffles the pack, after which the player to his right cuts the cards. These are then dealt singly to the players until each player has 13. The next card is turned up to start a discard pile. The remaining cards are stacked face down beside the turn-up to form the stock.

PLAY

The player to the dealer's left draws a card from the top of the stock or the top discard. He can then meld or pass before discarding a card to the discard pile. (A meld is three

Above: A player picking up the 3♦ or 4♦ could exchange them for the Jokers, enabling him to then use the Jokers in another meld.

Above: This meld could be laid down by a player with another meld on the table, but not as a player's first meld as it is worth only 32 points, which would be eight points short of the required 40.

or four cards of the same rank, or three or more cards in suit and sequence. No meld may contain two identical cards). If the top discard is taken, it must be melded on the first play. Play ends when a player melds all bar one of the cards in hand and discards that card. Each player's first meld must be worth at least 40 points.

Jokers can be used as wild cards, that is, they can represent any other card, in which case they take on that card's value. Once an initial meld has been laid down, its player can build on it by adding cards, or do the same with any other meld on the table. Jokers can also be exchanged for the cards they represent. If the stock runs out, the discard pile is shuffled to form a new one. If this, too, is exhausted, the game is declared void.

SCORING AND CONCLUSION

Losers score penalty points for the cards that remain in their hands. Aces count for 11 points, the three court cards and Tens count for 10, Jokers score 15 points and all other number cards score at face value.

At the end of each hand, the stakes are paid and the losers' penalty points calculated. Players with more than 150 penalty points are eliminated unless they choose to buy in. This involves paying a buy-in stake (the amount must be agreed by all the players at the start of the game) to the pool so that a player may remain in the game. They are allowed to do this twice, but only if there are at least two other players left in the game. The winner is the last player left and he is entitled to scoop the contents of the pool.

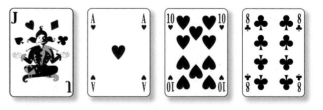

Above: A player left holding these cards at the end of a round would score a total of 44 penalty points: 15 points for the Joker, 11 points for the Ace, 10 points for the Jack, and 8 points for the Eight.

VATICAN

No one knows exactly where this game originated, though some card authorities think that it was probably a Czech or Central European invention some time in the mid-20th century. What makes it different from other Rummy games is the way in which melds are treated as communal. They can be arranged and rearranged more or less as the players please.

OBJECT

To be the first player to go out by playing all the cards in his hand to card combinations (melds) on the table. Melds are sequences or groups of three or more cards of the same rank, or in suit and sequence. In a group, the cards must all be of different suits. In a sequence, the Ace can be high or low, so King-Ace-Two is allowed.

THE DEAL

In the initial deal, the two packs of cards are shuffled together with two Jokers, and each player receives 13 cards. The rest are stacked face down on the table to form the stock. There is no turn-up and no discard pile.

PLAY

Each player in turn has the option of drawing a card from the stock or playing at least one card from his hand to any melds that have already been laid on the table. If the stock has run out and a player cannot play, he has no alternative but to pass.

Jokers are wild cards: they can be substituted for any other card, provided that, when one is played, its player states what card it represents. This cannot be changed unless the actual card is substituted for the Joker. After this, the Joker must be used immediately in a new meld.

It is illegal to draw and meld in the same turn. The first time players meld, they must begin by laying down a sequence of three cards of the same suit, all taken from their existing cards. Once they have done this, they can

Right: In Vatican, the first time that players meld, they must begin by laying down a sequence of three cards in suit, all taken from hand.

You will need: Two 52-card packs; two Jokers

Card ranking: Standard, Aces high and low; Jokers are wild

Players: Two to five, though the experts say that it is at its best with three or four

Ideal for: 10+

FIRST MELD

SECOND MELD

THIRD MELD

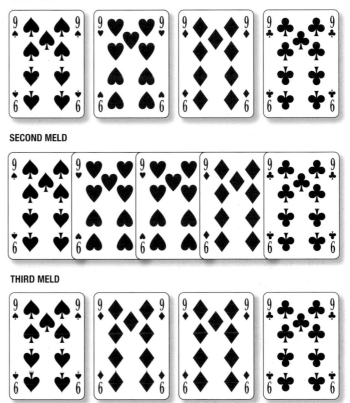

Above: The first meld here is legal in Vatican, but not the second or third. Five cards of the same rank cannot be melded, nor two of the same rank and suit.

then add more cards and rearrange melds to form groups and sequences at will. The one thing that matters in this game is that every meld laid on the table must consist of at least three cards of the same suit, or three or four cards of the same rank, all of which must come from different suits. More than four of a kind is not allowed.

CONCLUSION

If the stock is exhausted, players must continue to play if they can. Otherwise, they must pass. There is no system of scoring. The first player to run out of cards wins the game.

9 | BANKING GAMES

WHAT MAKES BANKING GAMES DIFFERENT FROM OTHER VYING GAMES IS THE NATURE OF THE VYING THAT TAKES PLACE. INSTEAD OF ALL THE PLAYERS COMPETING AGAINST ONE ANOTHER TO SEE WHO HAS THE BEST HAND, ONE PLAYER, THE BANKER, TAKES ON EACH OF THE OTHER PLAYERS INDIVIDUALLY. FOR THIS REASON, MANY BANKING GAMES ARE CONSTRUCTED TO GIVE THE BANKER A SLIGHT ADVANTAGE.

Many banking games require specialist equipment, such as a betting table marked with a staking layout or a shoe – a long oblong box with a tongue – from which the cards are dealt. To save time and effort, it is also customary to play with several packs of cards shuffled together, rather than just a single deck. Some games, however, can equally well be played off the cuff with a single pack of cards. There is no need to play using money – use counters or candies for a family game.

Banking games are quick to play and are essentially numerical, as suits are often irrelevant. Their widespread popularity is due to the combination of chance and skill. They are mostly defensive, not offensive, and there are two basic categories: turn-up games and point-card games. In turn-up games like Yablon, players bet on winning or losing cards as determined by a card or cards turned up by the dealer, and the bet is on whether a certain card will turn up before another. In point-card games, such as Blackjack, players draw cards one by one, with the aim of creating a hand of a given value, or nearest to that value. The objective in Blackjack is to achieve a hand with a total value of 21 or closer to 21 than the hand held by the dealer, but which does not exceed that figure. To achieve this straight off means being dealt a Ten, Jack, Queen or a King plus an Ace.

Above: Napoleon is known to have played Pontoon, among other card games, while he was held in exile on St Helena, from 1815 until his death in 1821.

PONTOON

This is the long-established British version of the internationally popular banking game Vingt-et-Un, or Twenty-One. Its origins go back at least to the early 19th century – when, to while away the time on the lonely island of St Helena, Napoleon's British captors taught him the game.

OBJECT

To get a hand that adds up to 21, or as close as possible without going over, preferably with just two cards.

SCORING

Number cards count at face value, while the court cards are worth 10 points each. An Ace can be worth one or 11 points. The best possible hand is a Pontoon, which is 21 points in two cards, followed by Five-card Trick, which is five cards worth 21 or less. A hand of three or four cards totalling 21 points beats everything but a Pontoon or a Five-card Trick, while hands of fewer than five cards and worth 20 points or less rank in order of point value. A player with a hand worth more than 21 points is bust.

THE DEAL AND PLAY

The banker deals a card face down to each player. All players bar the banker may examine their cards, then place their initial bets. Players can bet as many chips as they like up to an agreed maximum. When the players have made their bets, the banker looks at his card, and has the right to double. In this event, the players must double their bets. The banker deals another card face down. If any player has a Pontoon it must be declared, in which case the player

You will need:	52-card deck; gambling chips/counters
Card ranking:	See under 'Scoring', below
Players:	Five to eight is considered best
Ideal for:	7+

turns the Ace face up and stakes nothing more. If a player has two cards of equal rank, they can be split into two hands by placing them face up and doubling the existing stake. A player with cards worth 16 points or more may now stick, i.e. keep his cards and stake as they are, and the turn passes to the next player. Otherwise, he may buy another card, which is dealt face down, by adding a chip to his initial stake or he can twist without adding to his stake, when another card is dealt face up. This continues until all the players stick or bust.

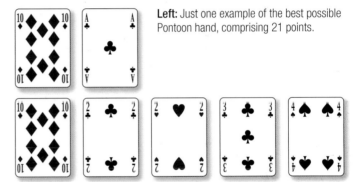

Left: Just one example of the best possible Pontoon hand, comprising 21 points.

Above: An example of a Five-card Trick which, in this case, adds up to 21 points, and is the second-best possible hand a player can have.

CONCLUSION

When all players have either stuck or bust, the game ends with the 'pay-off'. The banker's cards are turned face up, and the banker is free to add more cards to them, dealt face up one at a time, to attempt to bring his score to 21. At any point, the banker can elect to stick. If the banker has a Pontoon, the bank wins outright. If he sticks on a lesser hand, any player with cards worth more wins, and Pontoons and Five-card Tricks are paid double. If the banker goes bust, the bank pays players whose cards add up to 16 or more, the amount that they staked. If no one has a Pontoon, the used cards are added to the stock and a new hand is dealt. If there was a Pontoon, the cards are shuffled and cut before the next deal.

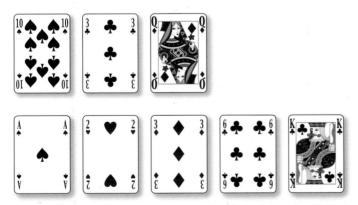

Above: Two examples of hands that have gone bust. In the first hand, an Eight was needed to make 21 points, but the Queen took the total to 23 points. In the second hand, a Five-card Trick looked like it was a real possibility, but the King takes the total just one point too high, at 22.

BLACKJACK

This is an extremely popular game, played in casinos around the world. Its origins go back as far as the 17th century to the French game called Vingt-et-Un. After the French Revolution, Vingt-et-Un migrated across the Atlantic to the USA, where it eventually took its current form.

> **You will need:** 52-card deck; gambling chips/counters
>
> **Card ranking:** See under 'Scoring', below
>
> **Players:** Any number, each playing alone against the House (dealer)
>
> **Ideal for:** 7+

OBJECT

To beat the dealer by building up a hand worth as close as possible to 21 points, but not over that total. If the player busts he loses, even if the dealer also busts.

SCORING

Number cards count at face value, while the court cards (known in Blackjack as face cards) are worth 10 points each. An Ace can be worth one or 11 points. A hand consisting of an Ace plus a court card or a Ten is a Blackjack, or 'natural'. It can win its holder a bonus, since he receives one-and-a-half times the original bet. All other winnings are equal. If, however, the dealer also holds a Blackjack, the hand is tied – this is termed a 'push'. No one wins or loses, and the stakes are carried forward to the next hand.

THE DEAL AND PLAY

Any number can play the game. The rules require all players to place their initial bets on the table before the hand can be dealt. Players simply put the chips they want to bet in front of them inside what is termed the betting circle. After the initial bets have been staked, the dealer deals two cards face up to each player and one card face up and one face down for himself. If a player is dealt a Blackjack and the dealer's turn-up is a number card between Two and Nine, that player is paid off immediately and his cards collected. If the dealer's turn-up is an Ace, court card or Ten, nothing can happen until the dealer's second card is turned.

If the dealer's turn-up is an Ace, a player can bet up to half the original stake that the down card is worth 10 points. In other words, he is betting that the dealer has a Blackjack. This is termed an 'insurance' bet, since it is worth double if it is correct. Similarly, if, after receiving the first two cards, a player thinks that he cannot beat the dealer's hand, he is allowed to 'surrender' – that is, immediately concede half the amount that has been bet. The exception is if the dealer has a Blackjack, in which case the entire stake is forfeit.

STANDING AND HITTING

Players dealt any combination of cards other than a Blackjack have two options. They can either stand (take no more cards) or call for a hit and be dealt additional cards. If the latter, these cards are dealt face up one at a time until the player either stands, or busts by exceeding 21 points. A player who busts loses cards and stake.

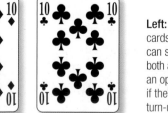

Left: Known as a 'natural' in Blackjack, this hand of 21 points wins its holder a bonus. The player receives one-and-a-half times the original bet.

Left: A player dealt two cards of the same rank can split them and play both as independent hands, an option often considered if the dealer has a poor turn-up showing.

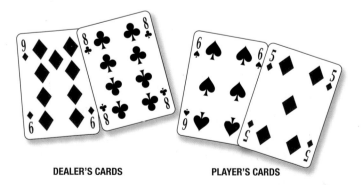

DEALER'S CARDS **PLAYER'S CARDS**

Above: The dealer's cards total an unpromising 17 points, while his opponent has 12 points. The player should hit for a further card here, in the hope of being dealt a card that takes his total closer to 21 than that of the dealer.

Left: Blackjack is one of the most popular casino card games in the world. Enthusiasts are attracted to the fact that success in the game requires a mix of chance with elements of skill. A lot of attention is given to card counting (keeping track of which cards have been played since the last shuffle).

Deciding when to hit or stand is key, as it can improve the odds of winning by more than 3 per cent. The basic rules are to stand on a hand of 17 or more and to hit on a hand of eight or less. If the dealer's turn-up is neither an Ace, nor a Ten or court card, he cannot make Blackjack. If it is a high card (an Eight or Nine), there is an increased chance he will go bust should he draw further cards.

Splitting

Players dealt two cards of the same rank have the option of splitting them and playing both cards as independent hands, though the same stake has to be wagered on the second hand as on the first. The player is then dealt a second card face up to each of them, and thereafter plays them as separate hands. There are two restrictions: if Aces are split, the player concerned can only receive one more card, while, in a split, a two-card 21 does not count as a Blackjack. Despite this, many players consider splitting to be worth doing if the dealer has a poor turn-up showing. In this situation, there is also the option of 'doubling down' (doubling the original bet). Players can also double down on any two cards.

Card Counting

Blackjack can be more rewarding than most casino games since it offers innumerable probability situations and choice of play. By keeping track of the cards that have already been played, a player can make a good estimate of the odds that apply to all the cards left in the deck. For example, the player can increase the starting bet if there are many Aces and Tens so far unseen, in the hope of hitting a Blackjack. If few Ten-cards have appeared to date, the fact the dealer must draw to 16 or less would

mean that his chances of busting are relatively great. Card counting is helpful when used in conjunction with sound basic playing strategy and a good betting technique.

Hard and Soft Hands, or Pairs

Any hand without an Ace, or any with one where the Ace must be counted as one to avoid busting, is defined as a hard hand. Experienced players always hit a hard eight or less and stand on a hard 17 or better. Soft hands are hands that include an Ace, which can always be counted as one. They are so-called because the chances of going bust are reduced. Players should almost always stand on a soft 18 or higher and hit a soft 17 or lower.

Pairs are two cards of the same rank. A player holding one has to decide whether to split the pair and play two hands rather than just one, or to play the hand as dealt as a hard hand. Aces and Eights are always split.

Conclusion

Once all the players have ended their turns by standing or going bust, the dealer turns his face down card face up. If the result is Blackjack, the bank wins the stakes of all the other players. If not, provided that the two cards now on display count for 16 points or less, the dealer can draw more cards, face up and singly. He must stand when the cards are worth 17 points or more.

If the dealer busts, all the players still in the game win. If a player's card count is closer to 21 than that of the dealer, that player wins. If it is less, that player loses. The only way a player can lose without busting is when the dealer is closest to 21.

BACCARAT

Anyone who has read Ian Fleming's *Casino Royale* will be familiar with the climactic game of Baccarat played between James Bond and the chief villain. The game probably originated in Italy in the 1490s. Its name comes from the word *baccara*, meaning 'zero', which refers to the fact that court cards and Tens are worth nothing.

You will need: 52-card deck; gambling chips/counters

Card ranking: See under 'Play', below

Players: Any number, each playing alone against the bank (dealer)

Ideal for: 7+

OBJECT

To beat the banker with a higher hand, the best possible being worth nine points.

THE DEAL

In Baccarat proper, the house is always the bank; in Chemin de Fer, a popular variant, it passes from player to player. Either way, the banker shuffles the cards and passes them to each player in turn, who deals two cards face down separately. The banker finally takes two. Players examine their cards and bet against the bank, which plays against each of them separately.

Right: It is the practice in Baccarat to deal from a shoe, but this is not essential.

PLAY

Number cards count at face value. Aces are worth one point. A two-card total of nine points is termed a 'natural' and cannot lose. A two-card total of eight is the second-best hand. No further cards may be drawn if a player is holding a two-card draw of six or seven. In hands adding up to more than nine, only the second digit counts, i.e. five plus seven is worth two, not 12.

If the count is less than five, a player must call for another card, which is drawn face up, but, if the count is exactly five, he may stand (take no more cards) or

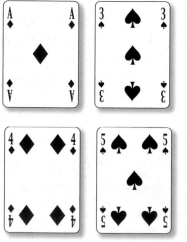

Left: If the two-card total of a player's hand is less than five, that player must call for another card, which is drawn face up.

Left: A two-card total of nine, such as that shown here, is termed a 'natural' in Baccarat, and cannot lose.

draw (call for another card). If the banker's hand is worth less than five points, he must draw. If it is worth three points, the banker draws if the opponent's third card is anything between an Ace and a Ten. If the banker's hand is worth four points, he draws to an opponent's third card between Two and Seven and, if it is worth five points, he draws to a third card which is between Four and Seven. If the third card is worth six or more, the banker draws only to a Six or a Seven.

Even with a hand worth just three points, the banker stands if the opposing player's third card is an Eight. If the banker has four points, the bank stands if the player's third card is an Ace, Eight, Nine or Ten, while, if the bank's cards are worth six points, the bank stands to an Ace or Ten. If the bank's cards are worth seven points or more, the banker always stands, regardless of the value of the third card a player may hold.

CONCLUSION

The hand with a value of nine points, or the one closest to nine, wins. If the hands are tied, there is no winner or loser, and the stakes are carried forward to the next deal.

YABLON

Also often known as Acey-Deucey and In Between, Yablon is a simple gambling game in which suits are irrelevant and only three cards are played per hand. In the USA the game has been recently rechristened Red Dog, which is confusing because there is another gambling game of the same name. Casino play involves anything up to eight packs dealt from a shoe.

You will need: 52-card deck; gambling chips/counters	
Card ranking: See under 'The Deal and Play', below	
Players: Any number, each playing alone against the bank (dealer)	
Ideal for: 10+	

OBJECT

To bet on whether a third card dealt by the dealer will rank between the first two cards.

THE DEAL AND PLAY

Cards from Two to Ten count at face value, Jacks score 11, Queens 12, Kings 13 and Aces 14. In Yablon, players bet that the third card dealt from the top of the pack will be intermediate in rank between the first two cards. All players make an initial stake, after which the dealer deals them two cards face up on the table with enough space between them for a third.

The dealer then places a marker to indicate the spread, the difference between the card values of the cards that have been dealt, and the odds being offered on an additional bet. If a player bets no further, but wins the hand, he wins the original stake at even money.

If they wish, players can now raise their bets, but not by more than the initial bet, the odds being determined by the 'spread' – that is, the number of ranks intermediate between the first two cards. For example, if the 5♠ and the 7♣ are dealt then the spread is one, and the players are allowed to place a 'raise' bet up to the size of the original bet. If the two cards are consecutive (such as the 5♠ and the 6♣), it is a tie. If they are identical, then the players are not allowed to raise. The number of players is irrelevant, since all players win or lose simultaneously. The only strategy decision that the player is allowed to make is whether or not to double the bet.

SCORING

The odds paid to successful players vary with the 'spread' – the number of ranks between the first two cards. A spread of one has odds of 5:1, a spread of two has odds of 4:1, and a spread of three has odds of 2:1. For spreads of between four and 11, the odds are even.

CONCLUSION

The dealer deals a third card face up. If the card is intermediate, the players win. If not, the bank does. Players who have raised and won get the original stake back, plus the raise at the appropriate odds.

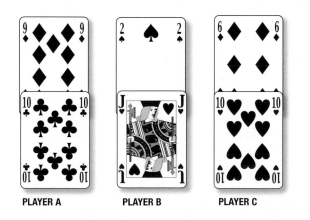

PLAYER A   **PLAYER B**   **PLAYER C**

Above: Players bet that the third card from the top of the pack will be intermediate in rank between the first two cards. For Player A, this is impossible, so he will fold. Player B has every chance of success, so he is likely to bet heavily. Player C's chances are limited, so betting will be more circumspect.

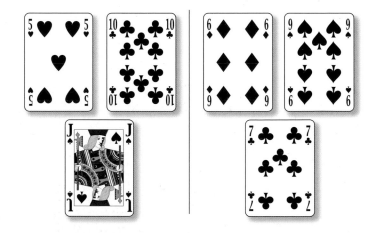

Above: On the left, the dealer has turned up a Jack outside the spread of the two cards dealt. All bets placed are lost. In the example on the right, the dealer's card falls in between the table cards, so any player who placed a bet and raised will retrieve his original stake plus the raise at appropriate odds.

SPECULATION

Mentioned by Jane Austen and Charles Dickens in their novels, this, according to the 1847 edition of *Hoyle's Games*, is 'a noisy round game that several may play'. In his *The Card Player*, published 20 years later, Charles Pardon described it as an ideal 'merry game for Christmas parties'. Though it dropped out of favour at the end of the 1800s, it is well worth reviving.

You will need: 52-card deck; gambling chips/counters
Card ranking: Standard
Players: Any number, each playing alone against the dealer
Ideal for: 7+

OBJECT

To end the game holding the highest trump card when all the cards being played have been revealed.

THE DEAL

All players begin with the same number of chips, each anteing one to start the pot. (The ante is the stake that each player must put into the pot before receiving a hand or new cards.) The dealer deals three cards face down in front of each player in a stack, turning the next one up in front of him to establish the trump suit. If it is an Ace, the dealer wins the game immediately.

PLAY

Assuming the dealer hasn't already won, players turn up their top cards, starting with the player to the dealer's left. If a trump card is turned up that is higher than the previous player's, its holder may offer it for sale or retain it. The holder of the highest trump card sits out play until a higher one is turned up. Any player may offer to buy any face-down card or cards sight unseen – they can be revealed only when turned up during play. If no trump card is turned up, the pot carries over to the next round.

Left: If the dealer turns up an Ace, he wins immediately.

Right: In some variations of Speculation, a player turning over a Jack has to pay an extra chip into the pot.

CONCLUSION

The game ends when all the cards have been exposed or if a player turns up the Ace of trumps. Whoever holds the highest trump is the winner.

Left: Writer Jane Austen (1775–1817) mentioned the game Speculation in her novel *Mansfield Park*, as did Charles Dickens (1812–70) in his novel *Nicholas Nickleby*.

LET IT RIDE

This banking game is a variation of the poker game Five-Card Stud. In Let it Ride, players do not have to beat anyone else's hand. It is popular with beginners because it is very easy to learn.

You will need: 52-card deck; gambling chips/counters	
Card ranking: See 'Hand Ranking' below	
Players: Any number	
Ideal for: 7+	

OBJECT

To construct a winning Poker hand, the minimum hand being a Pair of Tens. Players win according to how good a Poker hand is made by their three cards combined with the dealer's two cards.

THE DEAL AND PLAY

Each player places three equal stakes before the deal, although subsequently one or two of them may be withdrawn. Each player is then dealt three cards face down, while the dealer takes two.

After the cards have been examined, each player can either withdraw one of the three initial stakes, or let it ride – stay with their stake. The dealer then exposes one of the two cards he has been dealt and the other players get the same opportunity. This means that, at the most, players will have three stakes in front of them when the dealer's second card is turned and, at the least, one.

The skill lies in knowing when to let a bet ride. It is the best strategy to let it ride on the first bet if you hold a high-card Pair; Three of a Kind; three consecutive cards of the same suit valued Three, Four, Five or better; three of a Straight Flush with one skip – a missing card – and at least one high card, or with two skips and at least two high cards. On the second bet, in addition to the above, let it ride if you have Two Pairs, four of any Flush, four of a Straight or four High Cards.

SCORING

All players with a Pair or better are paid at the following fixed odds, according to their stakes

- A Pair – evens
- Two Pairs – 2:1
- Three of a Kind – 3:1
- Straight – 5:1
- Flush – 8:1
- Full House   11:1
- Four of a Kind – 50:1
- Straight Flush – 200:1
- Royal Flush –1,000:1

HAND RANKING

Hands rank from highest to lowest as follows:

- Royal Flush – A Straight Flush up to Ace; i.e. J♦, Q♦, K♦, A♦.
- Straight Flush – A combined Straight and Flush; i.e. cards in sequence and of same suit.
- Four of a Kind – Four cards of the same face value ('quads').
- Full House – Three of a Kind (also known as 'trips') and a Pair. When two players hold a Full House, the one with the highest-ranking trips wins.
- Flush – Five cards of the same suit. If another player holds a Flush, whoever holds the highest card wins.
- Straight – A sequence of five cards in any suit; e.g. 5♦, 6♣, 7♠, 8♥, 9♣. The highest Straight is one topped by Ace, the lowest starts with Ace. Should two players hold a Straight, the one with the highest cards wins.
- Three of a Kind – Three cards of the same face value; e.g. Q♠, Q♣, Q♥.
- Two Pairs – Two sets of Pairs; e.g. 10♦, 10♥ and Q♠, Q♣. If two players hold Pairs of the same value, whoever holds the highest cards in the two hands – the 'kicker' – wins.
- One Pair – Two cards of the same value, Ten or above; e.g. 10♦, 10♥ or Q♠, Q♣. Should another player hold a Pair of the same value, then whoever holds the kicker wins.
- High Card – A hand with no combinations, but having within it the highest-ranking card among the hands in play.

Left: On the second bet, it is best to let it ride if you have four of any flush.

CONCLUSION

The game ends after the dealer's second card has been turned with what's known as the payout. Players show their hands, and the dealer collects the stakes from any players whose three cards plus the dealer's two do not form a Pair of Tens or better. The others are paid according to their stakes at the appropriate odds.

10 | ALL FOURS GAMES

SOME OF THE MOST INTERESTING CARD GAMES IN THE ENGLISH-SPEAKING WORLD CAN TRACE THEIR ANCESTRY BACK TO THE TIME OF CHARLES II'S REIGN IN THE 17TH CENTURY, SPECIFICALLY TO A GAME CALLED ALL FOURS. THIS GAME INTRODUCED THE TERM 'JACK' FOR 'KNAVE', ALTHOUGH IT TOOK MANY YEARS FOR THIS NAME TO BE UNIVERSALLY ADOPTED. WHEN ALL FOURS REACHED THE USA 200 YEARS LATER, THIS SOON SPAWNED VARIANTS.

Despite its origins as a low-class game played mostly in alehouses or by servants and the lower ranks of the British Navy, All Fours rapidly became one of the most popular games in the USA in the 19th century. Despite subsequent competition from other games, notably Euchre and Poker, All Fours has survived, partly by developing more elaborate forms to compete with them for interest. It is the national card game of Trinidad and is still played in the Yorkshire and Lancashire regions of its British homeland.

Over time, quite a few variants of All Fours have developed including Pitch, Smear, Cinch and Don, all of which incorporate some system of bidding.

Pitch originated in the USA, where it is also called Setback or High-Low-Jack. There are two varieties: partnership and cut-throat. In the former, four players play in partnerships, and in the latter players are out for themselves. Smear is also American in origin and uses Jokers as extra trumps. Cinch comes from Colorado, and the aim is to play a trump high enough to beat the Five of Trumps.

Don is yet another version of the all-fours partnership game played in various forms in Ireland, from where it crossed the Irish Sea to reach Britain some time in the late 19th or early 20th century.

Above: The use of the term 'Jack' was considered rather vulgar when first introduced. In *Great Expectations*, Dickens has the character Pip divulge his social status when Estella says snootily 'He calls his knaves *Jacks*, this boy!'

ALL FOURS

The earliest reference to All Fours dates from 1674, when it was recorded in Charles Cotton's *Complete Gamester* as being a game played in Kent, England. From there, it migrated to the USA under the names Seven Up and Old Sledge.

You will need:	52-card deck; scorecards
Card ranking:	Standard
Players:	Normally four, playing for themselves or in partnership, though two or three can play as well
Ideal for:	14+

OBJECT

To win as many points as possible, thus being the first player to score seven.

THE DEAL

Players cut the pack for the deal: the one with the highest card becomes the first dealer. The deal passes to the right after each hand. Each player is dealt six cards, either singly or in two packets of three, and the next card is turned face up to indicate the putative trump suit for the hand. If the turn-up card is an Ace, Jack or Six, the dealer or the dealing partnership scores a bonus point.

ESTABLISHING TRUMPS

The player to the dealer's right has the option of accepting the trump suit, in which case he says 'Stand', or requesting a change by saying 'I beg'. If the dealer overrides the request, he says 'Take One', in which case the opposing player or partnership scores a point and play begins. If the dealer agrees to change trumps by saying 'Refuse the gift', the turn-up is set aside, each player is dealt three more

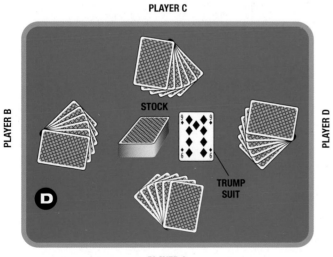

PLAYER C

STOCK

PLAYER B

PLAYER D

D

TRUMP SUIT

PLAYER A

Above: In this scenario after the cards have been dealt, the player to the dealer's right can accept the turned-up trump suit or request a change, in which case it is down to the dealer to make the final decision.

cards and the next one is turned up to find a new trump. The procedure is repeated until a new trump suit is established. If the deck is exhausted before this happens, the cards are 'bunched', that is, thrown in, shuffled and then dealt again. The entire process is termed 'running the cards'. Following it, players discard enough unwanted cards face down to reduce their hands to six cards again.

PLAY AND SCORING

The player to the dealer's right leads, and the other players must follow suit, or they must trump. If they cannot do either, they can play any card. The highest card of the suit led or the highest trump wins the trick. There are penalties for playing a card of a different suit to the card that was led when one could have followed suit, or failing to play a trump when one could have been played (termed a revoke or renege). If the offending player failed to follow a trump, despite holding one or more of the five top trumps, the penalty is to forfeit the game. For a revoke on a non-trump lead or failing to play a low trump to a trump lead, the opposing players win a penalty point and the revoking player cannot win the point normally awarded for game. Points are won in each hand as follows:

- One point for High (being dealt the highest trump).
- One point for Low (being dealt the lowest trump).
- One point for capturing the Jack of trumps.
- One point for turning up a Jack (if applicable).
- One point for Game (ending up with the highest total of point-scoring cards). Aces count four, Kings three, Queens two, Jacks one and Tens 10. Each partnership adds up the value of any such cards they have won in tricks, and whichever has the most scores the game point. In the event of a tie, no Game point is scored.

CONCLUSION

Play in each round continues until all cards have been laid. The first player to score seven points wins.

PITCH

This game, which is also known as Setback or High-Low-Jack, is played like All Fours, but with a round of bidding added. Instead of turning a card to establish trumps, the player who wins the auction chooses the trump suit, which is confirmed by 'pitching' – leading a card from the chosen suit to the first trick.

> **You will need:** 52 card-deck; scorecards
> **Card ranking:** Standard
> **Players:** Two to seven (four usually play in partnerships of two; six can also play in pairs)
> **Ideal for:** 14+

OBJECT
To win a specified number of tricks (rounds of the game) or to score bonus points.

THE DEAL
Each player is dealt six cards three at a time, and the remainder of the pack is placed face down out of play. The deal rotates clockwise after each hand.

BIDDING
Following the deal, there is a round of bidding in which each player can bid up to the maximum number of points that can be won in each hand for High (being dealt the highest trump), Low (being dealt or having captured the lowest trump), Jack (having captured the Jack of trumps) and Game (ending up with the most point-scoring cards). The bids are two, three and four, plus smudge, a bid to win all six tricks. Each bid must be higher than the one before it, though the dealer, who bids last, can 'steal the deal' by matching the previous bid. If, however, the other players all pass, the dealer is obliged to bid at least two.

PLAY AND SCORING
The winning bidder becomes the pitcher, with the right to choose the trump suit and lead to the first trick. The highest trump played wins each trick, or the highest card in the suit led. Players may use a trump on any trick even if able to follow suit. The trick's winner leads to the next.

A player or partnership that fulfils their bid scores the number of points they have won. Bidding two and making four, for example, scores four points. If they fail to make their bid, they are 'set back' by that amount, that is, they lose the value of their bid.

The opposing player or partnership makes whatever points they earn. If, for instance, the pitching partnership bid two, but their opponents take the Two of trumps, they score a point for Low. Likewise, High, Jack and Game are also worth one point.

PLAYER C

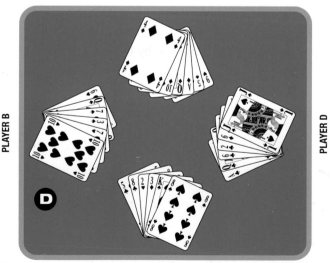

PLAYER A

Above: A scenario after the deal. Player C bids two in an attempt to win a point for High (highest trump) with his Ace. Player D bids three for the same reasons, plus he is hoping to win a point for Low (lowest trump) with his Two. Players A and B decide to pass. As the highest bidder, Player D pitches the Ace, thereby making Clubs trumps.

Left: Assuming Spades are trumps, if a partnership has bid two but its opponents capture the 2♠, the opponents score a point for Low (having captured the lowest trump).

CONCLUSION
The game is won by the first player or partnership to reach a previously agreed total of points – this can be as low as seven or as high as 21 – but this can be achieved only at the end of a hand in which the partnership made its bid. Paradoxically, this means that the game can be won by a partnership with fewer points than the losing partnership.

SMEAR

This game has four distinguishing features. First, two Jokers can be used as lowest trumps. Second, Low is always won by the holder of the lowest trump other than a Joker, not the winner of the trick containing it. Third, the Jick (the other Jack of the same colour as the trump suit) can be played as an extra trump. Finally, all players must discard after bidding is over.

You will need: 52-card deck; two Jokers; scorecards
Card ranking: Standard
Players: Four, in partnerships of two
Ideal for: 14+

OBJECT

To be the first partnership to score 52 points by winning tricks containing scoring cards.

THE DEAL

Players are dealt 10 cards each.

BIDDING

The deal is followed by a round of bidding, starting with the player to the dealer's left. Players can pass or bid the number of points (the minimum is four and the maximum 10) that they undertake to win in exchange for the right to name the trump suit. Each bid must be higher than the last.

PLAY

Once trumps have been called, the highest bidder picks up the 14 remaining cards, adds them to his hand and then discards 18 cards. The other players discard four cards from the hands they hold, so that everyone ends up with a six-card hand. A player with more than six trumps must play the excess number to the first trick: he may not include more than one point-scoring trump. The highest bidder plays first. The other players must follow suit if they hold any cards of the suit that was led. A player with no card of the suit led may play any card.

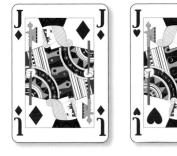

Left: The Jack of the same colour as trumps is called the Jick. So, if Diamonds are trumps, the J♥ is the Jick.

No trump may be played until all such cards have been played. The highest card of the suit led or the highest trump wins the trick.

SCORING AND CONCLUSION

Points are won as follows:
- One point for High, won by the highest trump.
- One point for Low, won by the lowest trump.
- One point for capturing the Jack of trumps.
- One point for taking the Jick.
- One point for playing either of the Jokers.
- One point for Game.
- Three points for Trey, won by the Three of trumps.
- One point for Game (determined by card rankings).

The game point goes to the team taking the highest total in scoring cards. Aces count four, Kings three, Queens two, Jacks and Jokers one and Tens 10. Each partnership adds up the value of any such cards they've won in tricks, and whichever has the most scores the game point.

Some variations do not recognize the Trey point, in which case the maximum bid would be seven, not 10. If the winners of the bid make as many or more points as they bid, they score all the points they made. If not, the amount of the bid is deducted from their score, which may leave them with minus points. The non-bidding partnership scores all the points they take in either case.

The first partnership to score 52 points wins; in the event of a tie, the bidding partnership wins.

Above: With Diamonds as trumps, a player taking a trick with the Three in it scores three points for Trey.

Above: Players score one point for playing either of the Jokers.

CINCH

This All Fours game, otherwise called Pedro, originated in the USA as a variation of Pitch. Though its popularity has declined, it is still widely played in various parts of the USA and Central America, with variants in Finland and Italy.

You will need: 52-card deck; scorecards
Card ranking: See under 'Play and Scoring'
Players: Four in partnerships of two
Ideal for: 14+

OBJECT

To be the first partnership to reach 62 points through taking tricks containing scoring cards.

THE DEAL

Players are dealt nine cards, three at a time.

BIDDING, DISCARDING AND DRAWING

Each player has one chance to pass or to bid. The minimum bid allowed is seven points and the maximum 14. If the first three players pass, the dealer is obliged to bid seven. The highest bidder announces which suit will be trumps, after which everyone bar the dealer discards their non-trump cards face down and is dealt enough replacements to give them six.

The dealer then discards, goes through the remaining cards and picks up all the trumps they contain. This may mean that he ends up with a hand of more than six cards, in which case more than one card must be played to the first trick, the card on top being the only one that counts.

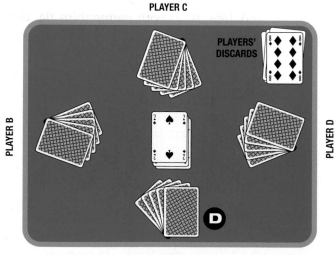

PLAYER C

PLAYERS' DISCARDS

PLAYER B

PLAYER D

PLAYER A

Above: As the dealer has the choice of taking any trumps from those cards left after the deal, he may have to play several cards to the first trick. Only the top card of those played by the dealer is considered to be in play, and he should end up with just five cards left in his hand.

The others are 'buried', that is, discarded and do not count. It is against the rules, however, to bury any of the scoring trumps.

PLAY AND SCORING

The highest bidder leads to the first trick. Players follow suit if they can or they can play a trump. If unable to do either, they can play any card. In the trump suit, cards rank Ace, King, Queen, Jack, 10, 9, 8, 7, 6, 5 (the Pedro), the other 5 of the same colour (the Low Pedro), 4, 3, 2. In non-trump suits the ranking is Ace, King, Queen, Jack, 10, 9, 8, 7, 6, 5 (when the opposite colour to trumps), 4, 3, 2. The highest card of the suit led or the highest trump takes the trick, its winner leading to the next.

If the bidding partnership makes their bid, they score all the tricks they take. If unsuccessful, they must deduct the amount of the bid from their score. The Ace, Jack, Ten and Two of trumps each score one point, while the two Pedros score five points each. The non-bidding partnership scores for everything they make. With the exception of the point for the Two of trumps, which goes to the partnership of the player who was dealt it, the partnership capturing the cards in tricks takes the points.

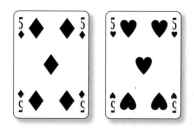

Left: In Cinch, the Five of trumps is called the Pedro and the Five of the same colour the Low or Left Pedro. So, if Diamonds are trumps, the 5♦ is the Pedro and the 5♥ the Left Pedro.

CONCLUSION

If both teams score 55 points or more, the situation is termed 'bidder goes out'. If the bidding team make their bid on the next hand, they win. If not, the hand is scored normally, the result being that the opposing team can often snatch the victory. The winners of the game are the first team to reach or exceed 62 points.

DON

Related to All Fours, this game probably descended from the 19th-century game Dom Pedro, which became popular in Ireland and America, where the name was abbreviated to Don.

You will need: 52-card deck; Cribbage board for scoring

Card ranking: Standard

Players: Four, in partnerships of two

Ideal for: 14+

OBJECT

To be the first to reach a predetermined score through winning tricks that contain scoring cards.

THE DEAL

Players cut to establish 'first pitch' – that is, who will lead first and set trumps. In the Irish variant, the player holding the 2♦ pitches or 'pucks out' to the first trick. The player to the pitcher's right then deals nine cards singly in the English version of Don or 13 cards in the Irish version. The remainder are stacked face down.

PLAY

All players now examine their hands, except the pitcher's partner, who cannot touch his cards until after the first card has been led. This is to avoid the risk of the player signalling to the pitcher the suit to make trumps. As in the majority of partnership card games, a player may not signal what cards he holds or what a partner should play.

The pitcher pitches a card to the first trick to start play, its suit establishing trumps. Players must follow suit if they can, trump or otherwise play any card. The highest card of the suit led or the highest trump played wins the trick. The winner of each trick leads to the next.

SCORING AND CONCLUSION

Because the scoring system is somewhat convoluted, it is the custom to keep score by pegging on a Cribbage board. Firstly, each side sorts through its tricks, when all cards have been played. They add up the points scored for winning tricks containing specific trumps or any five, and peg the amount on the board. In nine-card Don, they are scored accordingly: trump Ace = four, trump King = three, trump Queen = two, trump Jack = one, trump Nine = nine, and trump Five = 10. Non-trump Fives are worth five points.

Next, they add together the card values of the Aces, Kings, Queens, Jacks and Tens they hold in each of the four suits, to decide which team scores the extra points for 'Game' at the end of the play. The side that wins the majority of card points in that deal wins eight points. Here, Aces score four points, Kings three, Queens two, Jacks one and Tens 10. If both partnerships tie, then neither scores for Game. The first partnership to score an agreed total of points, customarily 91 or 121, wins.

In the Irish variant, scoring is the same except that the trump Nine ('Big Don') = 18 points; the trump Five ('Little Don') = 10 points and non-trump Nines score nine. The first partnership to score 80 wins.

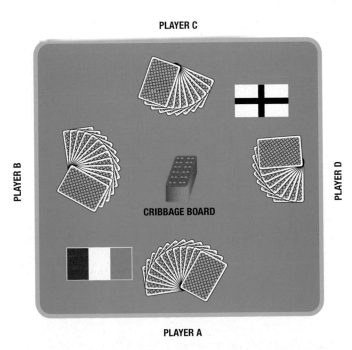

PLAYER C

PLAYER B

PLAYER D

CRIBBAGE BOARD

PLAYER A

Above: In the English version of Don, players receive nine cards; in the Irish version, 13 cards are dealt.

Above: The scoring trumps in Don are Ace, King, Queen, Jack, Nine and Five; the score is usually pegged on a Cribbage board.

11 | SOLO GAMES

THIS TYPE OF GAME DIFFERS FROM OTHER PLAIN-TRICK GAMES, SUCH AS BRIDGE AND WHIST, BECAUSE THE INDIVIDUAL PLAYERS ARE ULTIMATELY OUT FOR THEMSELVES AND FINISH THE GAME WITH A SCORE OF THEIR OWN. THERE ARE NO FIXED OR SET PARTNERSHIPS, ALTHOUGH IF FOUR PLAYERS ARE INVOLVED, TEMPORARY ALLIANCES CAN BE FORMED FOR CONVENIENCE – SOMETIMES THREE PLAYERS AGAINST ONE, BUT MORE OFTEN TWO VERSUS TWO.

Typically, the highest bidder in each deal names trumps and then sets out to win a specified number of tricks. The object of the other players is to prevent this. The bid is termed a solo. Its bidder is often known as the soloist and he leads.

Leading is often advantageous, since it determines the suit that the other players, if able, have to play. Playing last, however, has its merits as well, since the final player can react to what the previous players have played and, in theory, can compute the outcome of the trick for each of his possible plays. The contents of each trick are irrelevant – only the number of tricks taken by the individual players matters.

Some games have a remarkable historical pedigree. Ombre dates back to a 16th-century Spanish card game called Hombre, in which the term was used to denote the solo player. It is thought to be the most significant ancestor of subsequent bidding games, including Whist and Bridge. Boston, although its name suggests a link with the American War of Independence, probably started in France at the end of the 18th century.

Above: An English engraving entitled *A game of Whist* (c.1821), a classic trick-taking card game that was played widely in the 18th and 19th centuries.

Other noteworthy alliance games are Belgian Whist or Wiezen and Colour Whist or Kleurenwiezen, which is its more complex relation. Solo Whist, which developed in Britain into a popular game by the end of the 19th century, was derived from a Belgian game.

Solo Whist

Also known as English Solo, this game became popular in the 1890s, when it reached Britain from Belgium, where it was known as Whist de Gand (Ghent Whist). Players play for themselves, but they form temporary alliances – one against three or two against two – for each hand. There is no running score. Each deal is complete in itself.

Object

To make at least as many tricks (or, in the case of *Misère* bids, at least as few) as bid.

The Deal

Whichever player cuts the lowest card deals first. The deal, bidding and play run clockwise around the table. The cards are dealt in four batches of three with the last four cards being dealt singly to each player until every one has 13 cards. The last card is turned face up to indicate the prospective trump for the trick.

Bidding

The auction starts with the player to the dealer's left, each player having the chance to bid a contract, or to pass. From lowest to highest, the possible bids are:

- Proposal (or Prop) – a bid to win at least eight tricks in partnership with another player with the suit of the upturned card as trumps (scores one point per trick).
- Cop – an acceptance of another player's prop.
- Solo – a contract to win at least five tricks on his own

You will need: 52-card deck; no Jokers; scorecards or counters
Card ranking: Standard
Players: Four
Ideal for: 10+

(scores one point per trick).

- *Misère* or *Mis* – an undertaking to lose every trick (scores two points).
- Abundance – a contract to win at least nine tricks, with trumps of one's own choosing (scores three points per trick).
- Royal Abundance – a contract to win at least nine tricks, with trumps being the suit of the turned-up card (scores three points per trick).
- *Misère Ouverte* – a contract, with one's cards turned face up after the first trick, to lose every trick (scores four points).
- Abundance *Declaré* (or Slam) – a bid to win all 13 tricks solo (scores six points).

Play

Once the contract is established, the player to the left of the dealer leads to the first trick, except if a Slam has been called, in which case the lead passes to the soloist. In the *Misère Ouverte* bid, the soloist's hand must be spread face up on the table at the end of the first trick and before the second is led. Players must always follow suit if possible, otherwise any card may be played. The highest card of the suit that has been led takes the trick, unless trumps have been played, in which case the highest trump wins. The winner leads to the next trick.

Conclusion and Scoring

Generally, players settle up in counters or total scores at the end of each hand, when all 13 tricks have been won.

In Prop and Cop, each member of the winning partnership receives a counter for making the bid from both of the other two players, plus a further counter from both for each overtrick. If the contract is broken, each of the bidders pays five counters to the two other players for the failed bid, plus an extra counter to both per undertrick.

In all other bids, the successful soloist is paid by all three opponents, but pays them if the bid fails. The soloist wins three units in total (one from each opponent), for instance, if he makes a Solo, and nine if he makes an Abundance.

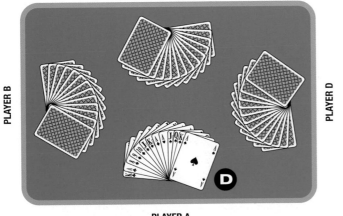

PLAYER C

PLAYER B

PLAYER D

PLAYER A

Above: This very strong hand, with Diamonds as trumps, is ideal for a bid of Slam: a contract to win all 13 tricks playing solo.

BELGIAN WHIST

Otherwise known as Wiezen, the Flemish for Whist, Belgian Whist is a descendant of Boston and is similar to Solo Whist. It is closely related to Colour Whist (Kleurenwiezen in Flemish, Whist à la Couleur in French). The difference between them is that in Belgian Whist the trump suit is established by turning up the last card to be dealt. In Colour Whist, it is determined by the bidding.

You will need:	52 cards; no Jokers; gambling chips/counters
Card ranking:	Standard, Aces high
Players:	Four
Ideal for:	10+

OBJECT

To make at least as many tricks (or, in the case of *Misère* bids, at least as few) as bid.

THE DEAL

Before the deal, each player puts an agreed number of chips or counters into a pool. The cards are then dealt four, four and five to each player. The last card to be dealt is turned face up to indicate the trump suit. The dealer picks it up when bidding is over.

BIDDING

In the bidding, each player can make a proposal, accept a proposal, bid higher or pass. The various bids, from lowest to highest, are as follows:

- Proposal – a contract to win at least eight tricks with the help of a partner (the caller has to take five of these tricks and the partner three).
- Acceptance – agreeing to a proposal, and thus to score eight tricks (at least three oneself) in partnership with the proposer.
- Solo – a bid to take five or more tricks.
- Abundance – a bid to take at least nine tricks, with trumps of one's own choice.
- Abundance in trumps – a bid to take at least nine tricks, where trumps is the suit of the upturned card.

- *Troel* – open only to a player holding three Aces, this is an undertaking to win at least eight tricks with a partner – either the player holding the fourth Ace or the holder of the highest Heart not held by the bidder.
- *Misère* – an undertaking to lose every trick, playing solo with no trumps.
- Solo Slam – a contract to take all 13 tricks.

PLAY

The player to the dealer's left leads, except in Slam or Abundance when the lead is with the soloist. Players must follow suit if they can, otherwise play a trump or any other card. In *Troel* with three Aces, the fourth Ace's holder must lead it to the first trick. If the bidder holds all four Aces, the highest Heart must be played.

SCORING AND CONCLUSION

The scores are totalled at the end of each hand when all 13 tricks have been won. A successful soloist wins the pool, plus a varying amount from the other players depending on the contract. The minimum is three times the contract's value. Partners divide the pool and win a set amount from their opponents. A losing soloist doubles the pool and pays the appropriate amount to each opponent. Losing partners double the pool between them and each pays the appropriate amount to one opponent.

Proposal, Acceptance and Solo bids score one for each trick, plus one for each overtrick. The scores are doubled if all 13 tricks are taken. Abundance scores eight points, *Misère* 10 points, *Troel* two points plus two per overtrick and Solo Slam scores 24 points.

Left: Comprising almost exclusively low cards, this hand is ideal for a bid of *Misère*: a contract to lose every trick, which is played in no trumps.

Left: With all four Aces, long Clubs, and only a slight weakness in Diamonds, this hand is worth a bid of Solo Slam, naming Clubs as trumps.

SOLO VARIANTS

Several solo variants exist, which are all fun to play and present a real challenge. Crazy Solo, of American origin, is a multi-player game – the number of players can vary from three to 12, which affects how it is played. A 36-card deck is used, but sometimes fewer cards are employed, depending on how many play. Knockout Whist is British in origin and it consists of seven hands of diminishing size.

CRAZY SOLO

OBJECT

To make more tricks than one's opponents, either in partnership with another player or alone.

You will need: 36-card deck, Twos to Fives removed

Card ranking: Ace, Ten, King, Queen, Jack (scoring 11, 10, four, three and two points respectively), followed by Nine, Eight, Seven and Six (each scoring no points)

Players: Four is ideal

Ideal for: 10+

THE DEAL

All the cards are dealt singly, starting with the player to the dealer's left, who also leads the first trick.

BIDDING

A round of bidding follows the deal to decide who will be the solo player, each bid having to be higher than the last. Players can bid Pass, Solo, Solo in Hearts, Go Alone or Go Alone in Hearts. In Solo in Hearts and Alone in Hearts, Hearts are the trump suit. Otherwise, the successful bidder calls the trumps.

PLAY

If the bid is Solo or Solo in Hearts, the successful bidder calls a card to choose a partner. The player holding that card does not need to reveal his identity until the time comes for the card to be played. The partnership is called the 'solo players' and their opponents are the 'gang'.

The player to the dealer's left leads to the first trick. Suit must be followed if possible or a trump played but there is no requirement to beat the previous card. A player who cannot follow suit or trump may play any card.

The highest card of the suit that has been led takes the trick, unless trumps have been played, in which case the highest trump wins. The winner leads to the next trick. The Ten ranks second, below Ace.

SCORING AND CONCLUSION

At the end of the game, points won by the caller and his partner are totalled to establish the margin of the win or loss. There are 120 points to be won, so scoring 61 or more of them wins the game.

The solo players receive points from (or pay) each member of the gang, the payout being calculated according to which suit was selected as trumps. If trumps are Spades, Clubs or Diamonds, then the payout is two points for every point over 60. However, if Hearts are trumps, it is three points. Each hand ends when all nine tricks have been won.

KNOCKOUT WHIST

OBJECT

To be the player who wins the trick in the final hand.

You will need: 52-card deck; no Jokers

Card ranking: Standard, Aces high

Players: Any number from three to seven

Ideal for: 7+

THE DEAL

Each player receives seven cards. The uppermost of the undealt cards is turned face up to indicate what the trump suit will be. The player on the dealer's left leads the first trick.

PLAY

Players must follow suit if they can, otherwise they may play any card. Each trick is won by the highest trump in it; otherwise by the highest card of the suit led. The winner of the most tricks in subsequent hands chooses the trump suit for the next. The second hand consists of six cards and so on until in the final hand, one card is dealt to each player.

A player who fails to take any tricks in a hand is knocked out of the game. If this occurs in the first hand, he is awarded a 'dog's life' – that is, he is dealt one card and can choose when to play it. If he is successful, he is reinstated into the game.

CONCLUSION

The game is won by the winner of the one trick on the final hand, or before that if one player wins all the tricks in an earlier round.

BOSTON

There are many versions of Boston, which won widespread popularity despite its extremely complicated system of calculating payments for bids, overtricks and undertricks. The game is a hybrid of Quadrille and Whist and may have originated in France in the late 18th century.

You will need: 52-card deck; no Jokers; scorecards
Card ranking: Standard, Aces high
Players: Four
Ideal for: 14+

OBJECT

To gain the most points by making no less and no more than the number of tricks bid.

THE DEAL AND BIDDING

Each player is dealt 13 cards. The player to the dealer's left opens the bidding, the highest bidder becoming the soloist, playing alone against the other three players unless one of them agrees to become an ally or supporter. The bids can be positive – an offer to win a stated number of tricks – or negative, in which case the contract is to lose them.

POSITIVE BIDS AND SCORING

Five is the lowest positive bid. This is an undertaking to win at least five tricks with a named suit as trumps. The supporter must win at least three out of the five tricks. If the bid is six, seven or eight, the supporter must take four tricks, that number remaining the same if the bid is nine, 10, 11 and 12. The highest bids are a Boston and a Boston *Ouverte*. In both, the contract is to win all 13 tricks, in the latter with cards face up on the table.

The former scores 100 points and the latter 200. Otherwise, starting from Five, the points that can be scored for each positive bid are: four (plus one for each overtrick or undertrick), six (plus two), nine (plus three), 12 (plus four), 15 (plus five), 18 (plus six), 21 (plus seven) and 24 (plus eight). Overtricks score if the contract is won. Undertricks score if the contract is lost.

NEGATIVE BIDS AND SCORING

The lowest negative bid is *Petite Misère*, in which the contract is to lose 12 tricks with one discard at No Trumps. It is worth 16 points, while a *Grande Misère* is a bid to lose all 13 tricks and is worth 32. A bid of *Piccolissimo* is a contract to take only one trick and scores 24. If the bidder holds all four Aces, the bid is Four-ace *Misère* and scores 40.

PLAY

The player to the left of the dealer plays the first card. Subsequent players must follow suit, if possible, or play a trump. Otherwise, they can play any card. The highest card of the suit led or the highest trump takes the trick, its winner leading to the next one.

CONCLUSION

In a solo contract, bonuses are added for overtricks and undertricks, plus the equivalent of two overtricks if the soloist holds three honours and four if four. The total is doubled if trumps are Clubs, trebled if Diamonds and quadrupled if Spades. The honours are Ace, King, Queen and Jack of Trumps. If the contract is supported, the total for each partner is halved. If only one member of the partnership makes the contract, he scores zero, while the losing partner loses half the value of his contract plus half the value of that part of the contract that has been won. Play ends when the final trick has been won or lost.

PLAYER C

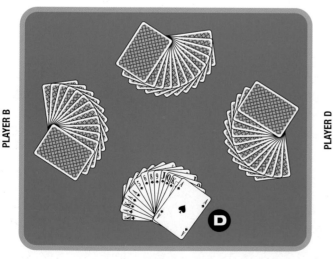

PLAYER B

PLAYER D

PLAYER A

Left: This hand, which is strong both in top cards and Spades, is perfect for declaring a bid of Boston *Ouverte*, naming Spades as trumps. The contract will be played with the bidding player's cards laid face up on the table, and will score 56 points if it is successful.

QUADRILLE

A four-handed adaptation of Ombre, Quadrille ousted Ombre in popular affection, only to be replaced by Partnership Whist. At least 160 chips of four different colours are needed to play it.

You will need: Standard pack with Eights, Nines and Tens removed; at least 160 gambling chips/counters of four colours

Card ranking: See below under 'Bidding'

Players: Four

Ideal for: 14+

OBJECT

To win at least six tricks after nominating trumps, either solo or in alliance.

THE DEAL

From the 40-card deck, the deal is 10 cards per player, usually dealt in batches of four, three and three.

BIDDING

Card rankings vary depending on the colour of each suit and whether the suit is plain or trumps. The top three trumps are *Spadille* for the A♠ (top trump), *Manille* (the Two if the trump suit is black or the Seven if the trump suit is red) and *Basta* (the A♣). They are collectively known as *Matadors*. The two black Aces are always trumps, regardless of what trump suit has been declared.

Each player takes it in turn to bid, pass or overcall – that is, to outbid a previous bid. In the simplest version of the game, the bids start with an alliance, in which the aim of the declarer is to take at least six tricks after nominating trumps and calling the holder of a specified King into a partnership.

If Solo is bid, the declarer proposes to win at least six tricks playing alone against the other three. *Vole* (slam) is a bid to take all 13 tricks without any support from a partner. A solo bid overcalls an alliance.

PLAY

The player to the dealer's left leads. Players follow suit if possible, otherwise they can play any card. However, a player holding a *Matador* (trump) need not play it to a trump lead unless it is lower in value than the led card.

SCORING

A successful soloist wins the pot, plus bonus chips paid to him by each opponent – four for the solo, one if he held three *Matadors*, two for double *Matadors*, one for *Premiers* (winning the first six tricks straight off) and two for *Vole*. If the contract is lost, the soloist forfeits the same number of chips to the other players.

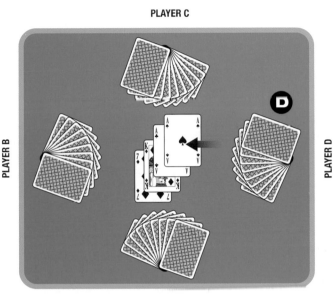

PLAYER C

PLAYER B

PLAYER D

PLAYER A

Above: Here, Player C looked set to win the trick after trumping with the A♣ before Player D played the highest trump of all, the A♠, and took the trick.

Losing partnerships divide losses according to how many tricks each partner won. If the declarer wins less than three tricks, he has to pay the total loss. The same goes if a player calls a partner.

If the declarer wins only five tricks, this is called *Remise*. If four or less, it is *Codille*. In the first instance, the declarer must double the stake and pay the opponents for any *Matadors* held. In a *Codille*, the stake is divided between the opposing players.

CONCLUSION

If the declarer wins the first six tricks, or *Premiers*, he has won the game. Alternatively, the declarer can decide to lead a seventh trick, in which case the bid becomes a *Vole* and all players must pay three more chips into a second pool. If the contract fails, the other players split this, but the declarer still gets paid for the *Premiers* and for winning the game.

OMBRE

This fast-moving trick-taking game was originally for four players – even though the player opposite the dealer took no active part in the game. It was therefore as a three-hander that the Ombre craze swept Europe until it was superseded by Quadrille. It was one of the first card games to introduce the notion of bidding, in which one player tries to fulfil a contract while the other two players try to prevent this.

You will need: 40-card deck (Eights, Nines and Tens removed from a standard pack); gambling chips/counters

Card ranking: See under 'Card Ranking'

Players: Three

Ideal for: 14+

OBJECT

The successful bidder aims to fulfil his contract by winning more tricks than any of his opponents. Their aim is to stop him by winning a majority of the tricks themselves, or to draw, in which case the bidder still loses.

CARD RANKING

The ranking of the cards varies with the colour of their suit and whether they are trumps. The top three trumps are called *Matadors:* the *Spadille* (the A♠), *Manille* (the Two of a black trump suit or the Seven of a red trump suit) and *Basta* (the A♣). The two black Aces are always trumps, regardless of what trump suit has been declared.

THE DEAL AND AUCTION

Before the deal, the dealer puts five chips in the pot. Each player is then dealt nine cards in packets of three. The remaining cards form the stock pile, which is placed face down on the table and used for exchanging cards.

Ombre has a language all of its own. The first dealer, chosen at random, is called backhand, the player to the right is forehand and the one to the left is middlehand.

Each hand begins with an auction. The winner of the bidding becomes the declarer (*Ombre*), and plays alone against the other two players (defenders) in partnership. The three calls that can be made in the auction are:

- Pass, in which case a player can take no further part in the bidding, and gives up his chance of being declarer.
- Bid, when a bid is made that outranks any bid previously made in the auction.
- Self, in which a player can equal a bid made previously by a player who is after him in rotation. Forehand can call self over the other two players, but middlehand can call self only over backhand.

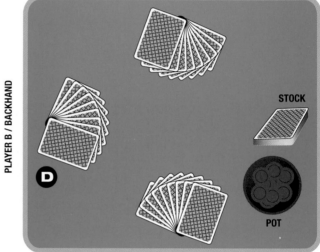

PLAYER C / MIDDLEHAND

STOCK

POT

PLAYER B / BACKHAND

PLAYER A / FOREHAND

Above: The dealer in Ombre is called 'backhand', the player on the left 'middlehand' and the player on the right 'forehand'.

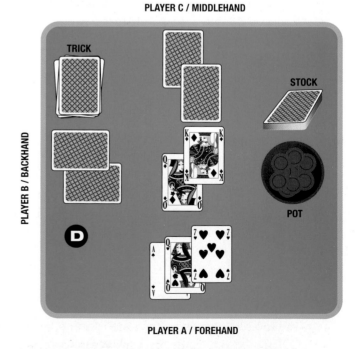

PLAYER C / MIDDLEHAND

TRICK

STOCK

POT

PLAYER B / BACKHAND

PLAYER A / FOREHAND

Above: Player A here can either trump by laying the *Spadille* (A♠), or renege with the 7♥. Doing the latter will leave the Queen a bare singleton, significantly reducing its chances of winning a trick.

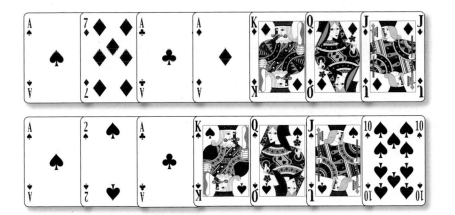

Left: With Diamonds as trumps, the top-ranking card is the A♠ (*Spadille*), followed by the 7♦ (*Manille*) and A♣ (*Basta*). In a red trump suit, the fourth highest is its Ace A♦ (*Punto*), but it is not a *Matador*. The remaining Diamonds follow in rank in descending order.

Left: With Spades as trumps, the top-ranking card is the A♠ (*Spadille*), followed by the 2♠ (*Manille*), A♣ (*Basta*), and then the remaining Spades in descending order, beginning with the King.

Only forehand and middlehand are involved initially in the auction, which ends when both players have called and one of them has passed. Backhand can then join in the auction, which continues until the contract is settled.

BIDDING AND CONTRACTS

The final bid by the declarer determines the contract. He plays either a Game or *Nolo* contract. In the former, he aims to take more tricks than either defender, and in the latter, he aims not to take any tricks at all. The players take turns exchanging cards with the stock pile, subject to restrictions relating to bids and corresponding contracts as follows:

- A simple game: the declarer names trumps, by naming the suit or turning the top card of the stock pile face up. All players can change their cards; the declarer goes first.
- A Spade game: Spades are automatically trumps.
- A *Tourné* or *Grand Tourné:* both game contracts, in which the top card of the stock pile is turned up. If *Grand Tourné* is bid, the bidder must hold *Spadille* (the A♠) and *Basta* (the A♣) in his hand.
- Solo: game contract where the declarer has to play his hand as dealt, but the defenders can exchange up to eight cards with the stock pile.
- Spade Solo: like Solo with Spades as trumps.
- Simple *Nolo*: *Nolo* contract. Only the declarer can exchange cards.
- Pure *Nolo*: like Simple *Nolo*, but neither the declarer nor defenders exchange cards with the stock pile.
- *Nolo Ouverte*: like Pure *Nolo* but when the declarer plays his first card, he also turns his hand face up for both defenders to see.

PLAY

Following the card exchange, the nine tricks are played. Forehand always leads to the first trick, regardless of who was dealer. Players have to follow suit if they can, unless one of them is holding a *Matador*, in which case he may choose whether to play it or keep it back and play a card from another suit. If the lead card is a higher *Matador*, a player holding a lower one must play it. The trick is taken by the highest card of the suit led or by the highest trump, the winner of the trick leading to the next.

SCORING AND CONCLUSION

Play continues until all nine tricks have been won. If the declarer wins, he takes the pot, and from each player:

- One chip for simple games and *Tourné.*
- Two chips for *Nolo*, *Grand Tourné* and Solo.
- Three chips for Pure *Nolo* and Spade Solo.
- Five chips for *Nolo Ouverte*

In Game contracts, the declarer wins outright if he takes the first five tricks. The alternatives are:

- *Bête*, in which the declarer scores the same number of tricks as one of the other players.
- *Puesta*, where no one wins a majority of tricks.
- *Codille*, when the declarer takes fewer tricks than one of his opponents.
- *Tout*, when the declarer takes all nine tricks. In this case, he has to declare the decision to try to do so in advance before leading for the sixth trick.

Winning *Tout* means the others have to pay the declarer an extra chip each. In the case of *Bête*, the declarer pays the other players according to which contract was bid. In *Codille*, there is an extra penalty: one chip for low contracts, two for Pure *Nolo* and Spade Solo and three for *Nolo Ouverte* with only the higher-scoring opponent being paid. If the declarer fails to win a *Tout*, he gives both the others a chip, but still gets chips for winning.

In Solo contracts, the declarer wins outright when he takes no tricks. The alternatives are:

- *Bête*, when one trick is taken.
- *Codille*, when the declarer takes two tricks or more.

PREFERENCE

This three-handed game is played in various parts of Europe, notably in Austria, Russia and the Ukraine, where it used to be the national game. Hearts is the highest suit, followed by Diamonds, Clubs and Spades. The game is played with either German-suited cards – a 32-card pack, the suits of which are Hearts, Bells, Acorns and Leaves – or a standard pack stripped of Sixes down to Twos. The main version of the game described here is called Austrian Preference.

OBJECT

To win at least the predetermined number of tricks. In each hand, one player (the declarer) chooses trumps and tries to take six out of the possible 10 tricks. The other two players (the defenders) try to stop this happening, but they are also obliged to take two tricks each. If a defender believes it will be impossible to do this, he is allowed to drop out of the hand.

THE DEAL

Players cut to decide who will be the first dealer, after which the deal passes to the right. The cards are dealt clockwise, three to each player, two face down on the table to form a stock, four to each player and then a final three. All three players put the same stake into the pot – in Austrian Preference, it is the custom to use money, rather than chips or counters. At the outset, each player contributes an equal sum to the pot.

BIDDING

The player to the left of the dealer opens the bidding. Players can either bid or pass, but if they pass they can take no further part in the auction. The possible bids are:

- One, two, three, four, representing Clubs, Spades, Diamonds and Hearts respectively.
- Game, which indicates that the bidder does not want to pick up and use the cards in the stock.
- Hearts, which is a Game bid in Hearts.

Players are only allowed to bid one higher than the previous bid or pass, so the first player to bid can only bid one, Game or Hearts. The other players can then bid two over the one, followed by three and then four.

You will need: 32-card deck (Sixes down to Twos removed from a standard pack); gambling chips/counters

Card ranking: Ace, King, Queen, Jack, Ten to Seven

Players: Three

Ideal for: 14+

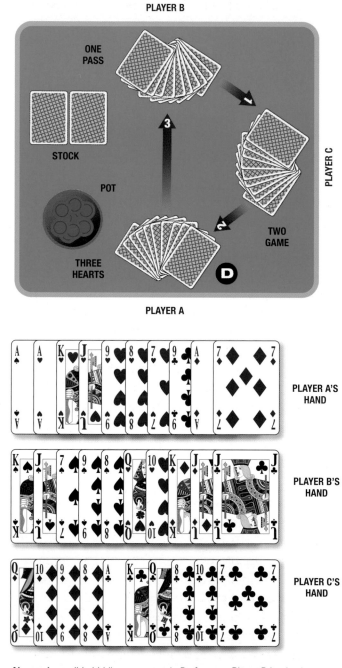

Above: A possible bidding sequence in Preference. Player B begins by contracting to make six tricks, but Player C bids higher, only to be outbid by Player A who goes higher again. After Player B makes the decision to pass, Player C then bids Game, forgoing the right to pick up the stock, but Player A contracts for Game in Hearts, the highest bid.

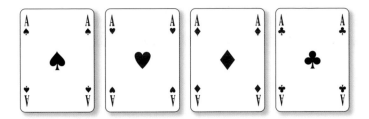

Above: A player holding all four Aces is paid an extra 10 points by each of his opponents if he wins the first six tricks.

Once game has been bid, only another bid of game or Hearts can outbid it. In the first instance, both bidders must declare what they are proposing as trumps. The one declaring the higher suit wins. If a player bidding a number is outbid, he can opt to hold. This is the equivalent to matching the other player's bid. If the second bidder does not raise the bid, the initial bidder wins.

A bid of one, if successful, means that the declarer can name any suit as trump. Two means that Clubs cannot be nominated, Three stops Clubs and Spades from being trumps, and Four means that Hearts are trumps.

PLAY

In a numerical contract, the declarer picks up the stock, adds it to his hand and then discards two cards face down. He then says what will be trumps, following which each opponent must decide whether or not to play the hand. If only one of them decides to play, he has the option of inviting the other to play with him, though it is his responsibility to win the four tricks the partnership needs, not that of his partner.

If both defenders concede, the declarer automatically wins all 10 tricks. If not, play proceeds with the declarer playing the first card of the first trick. The others must follow suit, playing a higher card, if possible. If not, they must trump or discard. The highest card of the suit led takes the trick, or the highest trump if any are played.

If, when both of the other players are defending, the first of them can beat the lead, he must do so with the lowest suitable card in his hand. This is termed 'indulging' and it provides the opportunity for the defending partner to take the two tricks he needs.

Failing to indulge when able to do so constitutes a revoke, when play stops and settlements are made without recourse to the pot. A revoking declarer pays the other players the equivalent of three-tenths of the pot, or five-tenths if only one defender was playing. If a defender revokes, he pays the declarer the full amount of the pot and four-tenths of its value to his partner.

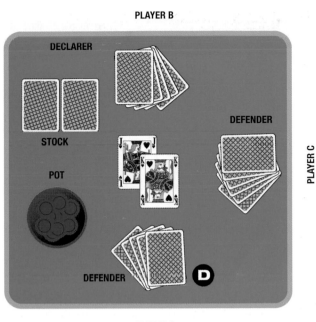

Above: With the declarer having led Hearts, the first of the two defenders, Player C, is obliged to beat the card if he can. Called 'indulging', it gives the defending partner the opportunity to take on the two tricks he needs to make.

SCORING AND CONCLUSION

When 10 tricks have been played, the players are paid from the pot according to the number of tricks they have made. First the declarer takes 10 points and pays any defender who did not drop out one point for each trick taken. If a declarer has taken less than six tricks, he pays a penalty of 20 points to the pot. The following bonuses apply, depending on the bid:

• Hearts bonus: in a Hearts game, a successful declarer receives an extra 10 points from each of his opponents, although he has to pay 10 to each of them if the bid fails.

• Four Aces bonus: a declarer who held four Aces receives a bonus of 10 points from each opponent if successful, but does not pay anything if he fails to fulfil his contract.

• No Ace bonus: a declarer who held no Aces and declared the fact before leading to the first trick, receives a bonus of 10 points from each opponent if successful, but pays them an extra 10 each if not.

ASSZORTI

This compelling three-player game was invented in Hungary. In many respects, it is similar to Preference, but it is simpler to play. Like many other Hungarian card games it uses a German-suited 36-card pack, the suits of which are Hearts, Bells, Acorns and Leaves, but a standard pack can be used when stripped of Fives down to Twos.

You will need: 36-card deck (standard pack with Twos, Threes, Fours and Fives removed); scorecards

Card ranking: Ace down to Six

Players: Three

Ideal for: 14+

OBJECT

To win at least the specified number of tricks bid. A bid is an offer to win at least six tricks after exchanging three, two, one or no cards with the stock.

THE DEAL

Players cut the pack to establish who deals first. Each player receives 11 cards, three each first then four batches of two. A further three cards are dealt face down on to the table to form a stock.

BIDDING

After the deal, players bid or pass in turn, starting with the player to the left of the dealer. If a player bids, he is undertaking to win at least six tricks after exchanging three, two, one or no cards with cards from the stock. Players are only allowed to bid one higher than the previous bid, or pass, so the first player to bid can only bid three. The next player can bid to exchange two and so on. The highest bidder becomes the soloist, drawing as

Below: Examples of the Hearts and Acorns suits in a German-suited pack of cards. The other two suits are Bells and Leaves.

many cards as were bid (if any) from the stock, discarding the same number and naming the trump suit or deciding the hand will be No Trumps.

ARRIVÁZS AND DOUBLING

If trumps are to be played, the soloist can also bid *Arrivázs*. This is an undertaking to win the last three tricks of the hand, for which he gets a bonus of eight points. This is doubled if the hand is No Trumps or if the tricks are captured without a trump being played. Game and *Arrivázs* are scored separately. Either or both can be doubled and redoubled up to five times, the levels being announced as *Kontra* (two), *Rekontra* (four), *Szubkontra* (eight), *Hirskontra* (16) and *Mordkontra* (32). If the soloist announces *Rekontra*, only the partner of the player who announced *Kontra* can respond by calling *Szubkontra*.

PLAY

Players must follow suit if they can, or trump if unable to follow suit. They may renounce, that is, play any other card, only if they are unable to do either. The player to the right of the soloist leads, the trick falling to the player of the highest card of the led suit, or to the highest trump if any are played.

SCORING

The basic scores for bids of three, two, one and hand are two, four, six and eight points respectively, the scores being doubled if the hand is No Trumps. Obviously, doubling and redoubling affects these basic scores. Over-tricks count for half the above values, while undertricks score minus the full values in the first and second possible bids and half values in the remainder.

CONCLUSION

Play continues until all the tricks have been won or the soloist has won six or more tricks.

OH HELL!

In this popular game, also known as Niggle, the objective is to bid to win an exact number of tricks – a player winning more or less is penalized. There are various ways of playing and scoring.

OBJECT

To win an exact number of tricks, no more or less.

THE DEAL

Players draw to establish who will deal first. If there are three or four players, the initial deal is 10 cards, if six play it is eight, while if seven play it is seven. (In the USA, each successive hand is dealt with one card fewer down to one, then one card up again back to the starting number. In Britain, the reverse happens, with the initial deal being just a single card.) The next card is turned face up to establish trumps and the remaining cards are stacked face down with the turned-up trump on top of the pile. The turn to deal passes to the left.

BIDDING

Bidding starts with the player to the dealer's left – the dealer always bids last. No player can pass, though a bid of *Nullo* (zero) is allowed. The dealer, however, cannot bid a number that would enable all players to fulfil their bids.

You will need: 52-card deck; no Jokers; scorecards

Card ranking: Standard, Aces high

Players: Three to seven players

Ideal for: 10+

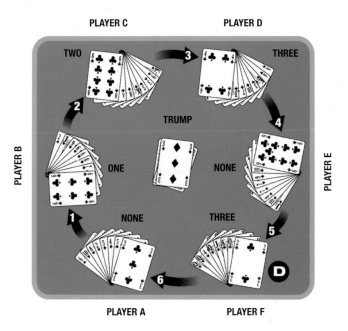

Above: A possible bidding sequence in Oh Hell! With six players involved, each receives eight cards, meaning that the final total of bids must not equal eight. Player F therefore, who is the last to bid here, cannot bid Two, so contracts instead to make three tricks. At least one player will fail to make the number of tricks he bids.

PLAY

The player to the dealer's left plays the first card, the other players following in turn. They must follow suit if they can, or, if they cannot, play a trump, assuming that they are holding trumps in their hands. Only if neither is the case can they play a card from any other suit.

SCORING

For making a bid, a player scores 10 points for each trick bid and won – just 10 points in total for a bid of zero. A player failing to make his bid has to deduct 10 points for each trick under the total.

CONCLUSION

Play continues until all tricks have been played and won. The final cumulative score decides the winner.

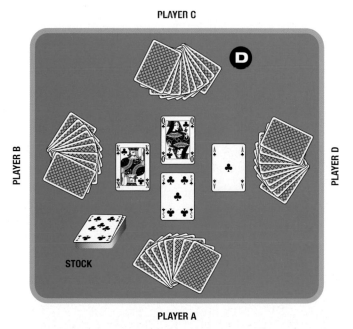

Above: Player D lays the A♣ to take the first trick in a round of Oh Hell! The game is also known by the name Niggle.

NINETY-NINE

Devised by British card authority David Parlett in 1967, this ingenious game revolves around its players bidding secretly, using bid cards, to win an exact number of tricks by removing cards from their hands. The suit of each bid card represents a different number of tricks: for example, Clubs represents three tricks.

OBJECT

To win exactly the number of tricks bid by discarding three cards representing that number. Players use the suits to represent the number of tricks bid as follows: ♣ = 3 tricks, ♥ = 2 tricks, ♠ = 1 trick, ♦ = 0 tricks. For example, a player bids nine tricks by laying aside ♣♣♣ (3 + 3 + 3 = 9), or three tricks by laying ♣♦♦ (3 + 0 + 0 = 3).

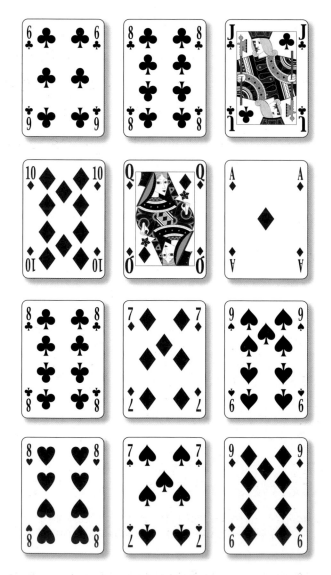

You will need: 36-card deck, (standard pack with Fives to Twos removed); scorecards

Card ranking: Standard, Aces high

Players: Three ideally, although can be two to five

Ideal for: 14+

THE DEAL

Assuming there are three players, each player is dealt 12 cards, three of which become bid cards. Normally, the bid cards are left face down until play ends. However, a player can decide to up the stakes by offering to 'declare' by exposing these cards at the start of play, or 'reveal' – that is, to also play with his actual hand exposed.

Only one player is allowed to declare or reveal at a time. If more than one player wishes to declare, the player nearest to the dealer's left has priority. An offer to reveal always supersedes an offer to declare.

PLAY

The first deal is played without trumps. Subsequent deals are played with a trump suit, which is determined by the number of players who fulfilled their previous contract. If all three did, the trump suit is Clubs, Hearts if two, Spades if one, or Diamonds if none. The player to the left of the dealer plays first. Players must follow suit, if possible, or otherwise trump or play any card. The highest card of the suit led or the highest trump takes the trick, its winner leading to the next.

SCORING AND CONCLUSION

Each player scores a point for each trick taken regardless of his bid, 10 points if all three players make their contracts, double if two players succeed and treble if only one does. A successful premium bidder scores an extra 30 for a declaration and 60 for a revelation. If the bid fails, the other players score the appropriate premium.

Play continues until all the tricks have been played and won. A game is 100 points with a further 100 being added to the winner's score. A rubber is three games.

Left: Players lay down three cards (bid cards) to show the number of tricks they aim to make with the nine cards in their hands. Each card in Clubs indicates three tricks, in Hearts it indicates two, in Spades one, and in Diamonds none. These four sets of cards from the top down, therefore correspond to: nine tricks (3 + 3 + 3 = 9); no tricks (0 + 0 + 0 = 0); four tricks (3 + 0 + 1 = 4) and three tricks (2 + 1 + 0 = 3).

12 | Piquet Games

Various factors make this interesting family of card games stand out. Points can be scored for various combinations of cards (which, in Piquet, is termed making melds). In addition, players make additional scores by taking tricks. Piquet itself is the oldest of these games, with a history that dates back to at least the 16th century, and a strong following among card game aficionados.

Though Piquet has a long and venerable history, its exact origins are somewhat obscure. What seems the most likely is that it originated in France, where its unknown inventor devised it to entertain Charles VI. It later became an English game by adoption from the time of Charles I onwards. Piquet is regarded by many as one of the best card games for two players, but its association with the aristocracy and literate upper classes, and the complexity of its rules may partly explain why it has lost its popularity since the end of the First World War.

In France, Imperial emerged in the 16th century as a two-player hybrid of Piquet and another old game dating back to the 15th century, known as Triomphe. It still has its adherents, particularly in the Midi region of the southern part of the country, and offers many points of interest to card game enthusiasts. Variants for three players or more became popular as well.

One of the earliest three-player variants is 'the noble and delightful game' of Gleek, an English game that reached the height of its popularity between the 16th and the early 18th centuries. Its name may be related to the German word *gleich*, meaning 'equal' or 'alike', for Gleek is the term used in the game to describe a set of three Aces, Kings, Queens or Jacks. Individual cards have unusual titles: the Ace is Tib, Jack is Tom, while Six, Five and Four are called Tumbler, Towser and Tiddy.

Above: *A Game of Piquet* (c.1861) by Meissonier. References to the game date back to 1534, making it one of the oldest card games still being played.

PIQUET

Modern Piquet can be played in two ways – American style and English style – though in practice there is little difference between the two. Two 32-card decks are usually used at a time – one in use and the other shuffled ready for the next deal. A game is known as a *partie* and usually consists of six deals.

OBJECT

To score the most points by capturing tricks and collecting card-scoring combinations.

THE DEAL

The players cut for first deal, after which it alternates between them. The dealer is called Younger and the non-dealer Elder. The former deals 12 cards for himself and 12 for the opposing player in packets of two or three, spreading the eight cards that are left over face down on the table to form a stock.

DISCARDING

The first stage involves the discarding and exchanging of cards, but, before this, a player can claim what is termed *Carte Blanche* if there are no court cards in his hand. This is worth 10 points. Otherwise, Elder discards up to five cards face down and replaces them from the stock.

Below: A standard pack of 52 cards is used in Piquet, but all of the cards below seven are removed – with the exception of the Aces. Of the remaining 32 cards, the Aces count for 11 points, followed by Kings, Queens and Jacks, which score 10 points each, and then Ten, Nine, Eight and Seven.

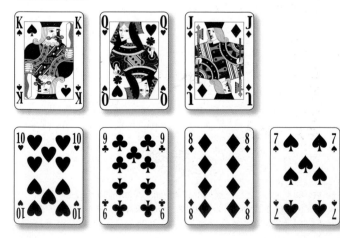

You will need: Two 32-card decks (Sixes down to Twos having been removed from two standard decks – see below)

Card ranking: Ace down to Seven

Players: Two

Ideal for: 14+

American rules say this is optional, but English ones state that at least one card must be discarded. Younger may then discard and exchange up to as many cards as are left in the stock, but he has the freedom to decline to do so. If Younger does discard and exchange any cards, he may then inspect any remaining cards in the stock, but this means Elder can inspect them as well. Both players may examine their own discards at any stage during play.

DECLARING COMBINATIONS

Depending on their cards, both players can declare three types of combination, namely:

- A point, which is a collection of cards all of the same suit.
- A sequence, which is a run of three or more cards in one suit in rank order.
- A meld, when a player holds three or four cards of the same rank but in different suits.

It is not obligatory to announce the best combination – or to declare a weak one – if the player concerned believes that such concealment will serve his tactics the better. This is termed 'sinking a declaration'.

Elder declares first, announcing his best combinations in each category, saying 'A point of…', 'A sequence of…' or, in the case of a meld, 'A three or four of…'. After each announcement, Young says 'good', meaning that Elder's hand is better and can be scored, 'not good' if Younger has a better combination, or 'equal', in which case the points go to the player with the higher-ranking cards. Aces score 11; the court cards and Tens 10 each; and Nines, Eights and Sevens their face value.

PLAYING

Once the declarations have been completed, Elder announces the score he has made thus far and leads to the first trick, scoring an extra point for leading. Younger responds by announcing his total score. If he has failed to score anything and Elder's score reaches 30 as the result of leading to the trick, the Elder wins a *pique*, a bonus of 30 points. Elder then plays the first card to the next trick. Younger follows suit, if possible, or otherwise discards. Trumps do not feature in Piquet. Players must follow suit. Each trick is worth a point if the player who led to it wins it, otherwise it is worth two. A player taking seven to 11 tricks gets a bonus of 10 points 'for cards', while taking all 12 tricks means a bonus of 40 'for *Capot*'. Winning the last trick scores an extra point.

SCORING

In a point combination, the player with the longest suit scores a point for each card in it. Thus:

- Point of three scores three.
- Point of four scores four.
- Point of five scores five.
- Point of six scores six.
- Point of seven scores seven.
- Point of eight scores eight.

Scoring for sequences is as follows:

- A *Tierce* (three cards) scores three.
- A *Quart* (four) scores four.
- A *Quint* (five) scores 15.
- A *Sixième* (six) scores 16.
- A *Septième* (seven) scores 17.
- A *Huitième* (eight) scores 18.

Scores for melds are as follows (sets of Nines, Eights and Sevens do not count):

- *Quatorze* (four Aces, Kings, Queens, Jacks or Tens) scores 14.
- *Trio* (three Aces, Kings, Queens, Jacks or Tens) scores three.

If a player scores 30 points before the other has scored, he is awarded a bonus of 60 points. This is a *repique*.

CONCLUSION

At the end of the sixth deal, the scores are totalled. If a player has scored under 100 points, he is deemed to be 'Rubiconed'. His opponent wins and scores 100 plus the two final scores. If a player has scored more than 100 points, he 'crosses the Rubicon' and wins the game, scoring 100 plus the difference between the two final totals. In a tie, two more deals are played as a tiebreaker.

Right: Piquet became a popular card game among the aristocracy in England during the reign of Charles I (1625–49).

Above: An unbeaten set of four Queens is known as a *Quatorze* and is worth a total of 14 points to its holder.

Above: Elder's starting and finishing hands before and after discarding his cards. Elder has so many weak cards in his hand that it is worth exchanging the maximum five cards for five new ones.

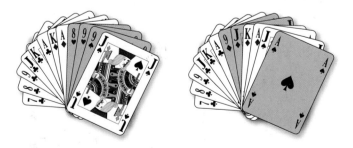

Above: Younger's starting and finishing hands. After Elder discards five cards, Younger is left with three cards to exchange with those from the stock in the hope of picking up some better ones.

IMPERIAL

In this game, players use counters to keep score. Each player starts with five red counters and six white to their left, moving one of the white ones to the right to signify each point won in play. Six points equals an imperial. This is marked by a red counter and the six white counters are moved back again to the left.

OBJECT

To score the most points by capturing tricks and collecting point-scoring card combinations.

THE DEAL

The dealer deals two hands of 12 cards each in packets of two, three or four. The next card is turned face up to establish trumps. The remaining cards are placed face down across it. If the turn-up is an 'honour card' (an Ace, King, Queen, Jack or Seven) the dealer scores a point for it. If it is an Ace or a King, the dealer can exchange a Seven for it, assuming that he holds one in his hand.

PLAY AND SCORING

Before play starts, both players work out and announce how many points they have according to the values of the cards they hold in any one suit. An Ace scores 11, the court cards 10 each and the Ten, Nine, Eight and Seven

> **You will need:** 32-card deck, Sixes down to Twos having been removed; red and white counters
>
> **Card ranking:** Ace down to Seven
>
> **Players:** Two
>
> **Ideal for:** 14+

are at face value. The player with the higher score wins a point, but, if the scores are tied, the point goes to the non-dealing player. Both players also score any *Impériales* they may be holding in their hand, which can be:

- An *Impériale d'Alout* (King, Queen, Jack and Ten), worth 12 points if they are trumps, six points if they are non-trumps.
- An *Impériale d'Honneur* (all four of one of the following ranks plus one of the other cards: Ace, King, Queen, Jack or Seven), worth six points.
- An *Impériale Blanche* (all four cards of any rank other than court cards with one other card, again not a court card), worth 12 points.

They must be declared strictly in the above order and shown if the opposing player requests it.

After the *Impériales* have been declared, play begins with the non-dealing player leading. The dealer must follow suit with a higher card, play a trump or revoke if unable to do either. The trick is taken by the highest card of the suit led or the highest trump if any are played. The winner of each trick leads to the next.

A player scores a point for leading an honour to a trick and one for capturing a trick containing one. At the end of play, a player winning more than six tricks scores a point for each of them. If one player takes all 12 tricks, this is *Capot*, which is worth 12 points, but, if the tricks are divided, neither player scores.

Whenever a player scores six points, the opposing player's points are forfeited. The sole exception is when an *Impériale Blanche* is declared, when the opposing player's points are not forfeited. Scores can be written down but counters are preferable.

HAND 1

HAND 2

HAND 3

Above and left: Examples of scoring Imperials: (1) An *Impériale d'Alout*, worth 12 points in trumps or otherwise six points (2) an *Impériale d'Honneur*, worth six points and (3) an *Impériale Blanche*, worth 12 points.

CONCLUSION

Game is 36 points. The first player to shift all 11 counters from left to right is the winner.

GLEEK

This is a somewhat elaborate game in which there are four main stages. In the first, players bid for the chance to improve their hands by discarding cards and replacing them with ones from the stock. They then bet as to who holds the longest suit, followed by declarations of Gleeks (Three of a Kind) and Mournivals (Four of a Kind) before getting down to the final stage of trick play.

OBJECT

To score the most points by capturing tricks and collecting certain cards or card-scoring combinations.

THE DEAL

The players cut the pack to establish who will be the dealer. The lowest card wins. Each of the players is dealt 12 cards in packets of four, the remaining cards being placed face down to form the stock. Players put an equal number of chips into a pot. The dealer turns up the top card of the stock to establish trumps.

BIDDING

All players start with the same number of chips. After the deal has been completed, they bid for the right to discard seven cards in exchange for the stock, although the turned-up trump is excluded. The player to the dealer's left bids first, starting the bidding with 10 chips. The other players can either raise the bid by two chips or pass, so dropping out of the bidding. When two players have passed, the winning bidder pays half the final bid to each of them. Without showing any cards, he discards seven cards and replaces them with the stock.

VYING

The players now bet to see who holds the best 'ruff' – the highest card value in a single suit. This is determined by adding up the cards. Aces count 11, Kings, Queens and Jacks 10 each and all the other cards at face value. The players start by putting two chips each into a pot, after

You will need: 44-card deck (Threes and Twos removed from a standard pack); scorecards; gambling chips/counters

Card ranking: Ace down to Four

Players: Three

Ideal for: 14+

which they have several options. They can pass, decide to match the previous bet, or raise it by a further two chips. The process continues until two players pass or there is a showdown. The holder of the best hand wins the pot.

Finally, all the players declare and score for any Gleeks and Mournivals they may hold, each opposing player paying the holder the appropriate number of chips. In Gleeks, Aces are worth four chips, Kings three, Queens two and Jacks one. In Mournivals, Aces are worth eight chips, Kings six, Queens four and Jacks two.

PLAYING THE TRICKS

The player to the left of the dealer leads. Players must follow suit if possible, trump or otherwise play any card. The highest trump or the highest card of the suit led wins the trick, and the winner leads to the next.

Every trick taken scores three points for its winner, plus bonus points for the top trumps. These have their own names and special point values. An Ace is Tib and worth 15 points, Kings and Queens score three points each, a Jack is Tom and worth nine points, while Six (Tumbler), Five (Towser) and Four (Tiddy) score six, five and four points respectively. Tumbler and Towser are optional inclusions. If the turned-up card is an Ace or any of the court cards, the dealer counts it in as part of his total score.

CONCLUSION

A game consists of 12 tricks. At the end, any player scoring less than 22 puts a chip into the pot for every point of the shortfall, while any player scoring more than 22 takes a chip out of the pot for every point scored in excess of that figure.

Left: The top trumps won in tricks (here, assuming trumps are Spades) have their own names and special point values. An Ace is known as Tib and is worth 15 points, Kings and Queens are each worth three points, a Jack (Tom) scores nine points, while Six, Five, Four, known as Tumbler, Towser and Tiddy respectively, score just their face value.

Glossary

A

Aces High The term used when the Ace is the highest-ranked card in each suit. When it is the lowest-ranked, the term is **Aces Low**.

Alliance A temporary partnership between players that lasts for only one deal.

Ante In gambling games, the opening stake that all players must make before or at the start of each deal.

Auction Bidding to establish which suit should be trumps, how many tricks the bidders undertake to win and other basic conditions of a particular game.

B

Bid The offer to win a certain number of tricks in exchange for choosing conditions of play, for example, what the trump suit will be. If a bid is not overcalled by a higher one, then it becomes a contract.

Blank A term used in card-point games to describe a card that is valueless.

Boodle In the game Michigan, cards from a separate pack placed on a layout on which bets (gambling chips or counters) are staked.

Book In Bridge and Whist, the first six tricks won by a side, which are recorded 'below the line'. In collecting games, a set of four cards of the same rank.

C

Card-points The point-scoring values of specific cards, principally in point-trick games. These points are different to the nominal face values.

Carte blanche A hand containing no court cards.

Carte rouge A hand in which every card counts towards a scoring combination.

Chip Counter which is used to represent money. Also called a gambling chip.

Combination A set of scoring cards that match each other in rank or by suit.

Court cards The King, Queen and Jack of each suit, as opposed to the numbered or 'pip' cards. They are also sometimes referred to as picture cards.

Cut To divide a pack of playing cards by lifting a portion from the top, to establish who deals first.

D

Deadwood Penalty cards remaining in opponents' hands when a player goes out.

Deal The distribution of cards to the players at the beginning of a game and the play ensuing between one deal and the next.

Declare To state the contract or conditions of play (for example, the trump suit or number of tricks intended, etc.). To reveal your hand and score for achieving a particular combination of cards.

Declarer The highest bidder in an auction, who then tries to fulfil his contract.

Deuce The Two of any suit.

Discard A card that a player has rejected and placed on a discard pile. To throw away a worthless or unwanted card to a trick.

Draw To take or be dealt one or more cards from a stock or discard pile.

Dummy A full hand of cards dealt to the table, or, in Bridge, to one of the players (who has to spread them face up on the table at a certain point in the game), with which the declarer plays as well as with his own hand.

E

Elder/Eldest The player who is obliged to lead, bid or make the opening bet first, usually the person seated to the left of the dealer in left-handed games, or seated to the right in right-handed games.

Exchange To discard cards and receive the same number of replacements or to add cards to a hand and then discard the same number.

F

Flush A hand of cards that are all of the same suit.

Follow suit To play a card of the same suit as the last one played.

G

Game The whole series of deals, or the target score. For example, 'game is 500 points'.

Game points Card points that are won to fulfill a particular bid.

Go out To play the last card of a hand.

H

Hand The cards held by each player or the play that takes place between one deal and the next.

Head To play a higher card than any so far played to the trick.

Hole cards The cards dealt face down to each player which remain unseen by the other players, until the end of the game.

Honours Cards that attract bonus scores or extra payments if they are held in hand and, occasionally, if captured in play.

J

Joker An extra card supplied with the standard 52-card pack that is often used as a wild card.

K

Kitty Another term for the pool or pot of chips that are being played for.

Knock In Rummy, a player uses this to signify that all his cards are melded. In Poker, knocking can be used to signify that a player will make no more bets.

L

Laying off The playing of cards to opponents' melds on the table in Rummy games.

Lead The first card to be played or the action of playing the first card.

M

Maker The player who names the trump suit.

Marriage A meld of the King and Queen of the same suit.

Meld A group of cards of the same rank or in sequence that attracts scores or privileges.

Misdeal To deal cards incorrectly, in which case they must be collected, shuffled and dealt again.

Misère A contract to lose every trick in a hand, otherwise termed a *Null*.

N

Null A contract to lose every trick in a hand, or a card carrying no point value in point-trick games.

O

Ouverte A contract played with one's hand of cards spread face up on the table for everyone to see.

Overcall To bid higher than the previous bidder.

Overtrick A trick taken in excess of the number a player is contracted to take.

P

Pair Two cards of the same rank.

Pass To miss a turn when it comes to bidding or playing without dropping out of play.

Plain suit A suit other than the trump suit.

Pool/Pot This is a sum of money or an agreed equivalent, such as a number of chips, to which the players contribute before play starts or throughout play and which is taken by the eventual winner.

Prial Three cards of the same rank; a triplet.

Q

Quint In Piquet, a set of five cards.
In Quinto, the Five of every suit, and every pair of cards in a suit that totals five. In this game, the Joker is known as the Quint Royal.

R

Raise In Poker, to increase the level of a bet, usually by calling the previous bet and then wagering at least the same amount again.

Rank A card's denomination and its relative trick-taking power (for example, 'Ace ranks above King').

Renege To fail to follow suit to the card led, but legally, in accordance with the rules of the game.

Revoke To fail to follow suit, when able and required to do so. It usually incurs a penalty if detected.

Round A division of play in which every player participates in dealing, bidding, playing a trick, etc. the same number of times (usually once).

Rubber In partnership games, a match usually consisting of three games and thus won by the side winning two.

Ruff In games of Bridge, playing a trump card on a trick that was led with a plain suit. In Gleek, it is the highest card value a player holds in a single suit

Run Another term for a sequence.

S

Sequence A run of three or more cards of the same suit in rank or numerical order.

Shoe A box from which cards are dealt in some card games.

Slam A bid to win every trick in a hand.

Solo A contract played with the hand as dealt without exchanging any cards, or, played alone against the other players. The soloist is the player who elects to play alone.

Stake The amount of money or chips a player is willing to play with during a game, or the amount a player needs to be included in a game.

Stock The cards that are not dealt immediately to the players, but may be dealt or drawn from later on during the game.

Suit The internationally recognized suits are Hearts, Clubs, Diamonds and Spades. There are also local ones found in German Italian and Spanish games.

T

Talon The undealt portion of the pack put aside for use later in a game; the same as the stock.

Three of a Kind Three cards of the same rank.

Trey The Three of any suit.

Trick A round of cards, consisting of one from each player in turn, played according to the rules of the particular game.

Trump A suit that outranks all the others. A trump card always beats any card from a plain suit.

Turn-up A card, also called the upcard, turned up at the start of play to determine which suit is trumps and, depending on the game, at other times during play for a variety of reasons.

U

Undertrick A trick which is less than the number bid or contracted.

Upcard Another term for the turn-up card.

V

Void Having no cards of a specified suit.

Vole The winning of every trick; same as slam.

Vulnerable In Bridge, this describes a partnership, which, having won one game towards the rubber, is subject to increased scores or penalties.

W

Waste pile A pile of unwanted cards, usually dealt face up.

Widow A hand of cards dealt to the table face down usually at the start of play which players may exchange cards with during the game.

Wild card A card that can stand in for any other card, either played freely or subject to certain restrictions, depending on the game.

Y

Younger/Youngest The player last in turn to bid or play at the beginning of a game.

INDEX